The Complete Guide to

GLASS
PAINTING

The Complete Guide to
GLASS
PAINTING

OVER 90 TECHNIQUES WITH 25 ORIGINAL PROJECTS AND 400 MOTIFS

ALAN D. GEAR AND BARRY L. FREESTONE

COLLINS & BROWN

For David Launcelot

First published in Great Britain in 2000 by
Collins & Brown Limited
London House
Great Eastern Wharf
Parkgate Road
London SW11 4NQ

1 3 5 7 9 8 6 4 2

British Library Cataloguing-in-Publication Data:
A catalogue record for this book
is available from the British Library.

ISBN 1 85585 950 5

Conceived, edited and designed by
Collins & Brown Limited

Editor: Kate Haxell
Designer: Roger Daniels
Design conceived by: Christine Wood
Photography: Matthew Dickens
Illustrations: Dominic Harris

Reproduction by Classic Scan Ltd
Printed and bound in China by Dai Nippon
Printing Co Ltd

Distributed in the United States and Canada by
Sterling Publishing Co,
387 Park Avenue South, New York,
NY10016, USA

Contents

Introduction

When we first started glass painting some twenty years ago, there were no books, no videos, no courses – nothing. Today, to our joy and amazement, glass painting is one of the most enjoyed and rapidly developing crafts in this country and it is attracting more and more people of all ages every year. As well as selling glass painting supplies, our company, Rainbow Glass, runs teaching workshops, and they are always over-subscribed; our youngest-ever pupil was eight and our eldest was well into her eighties.

In this book, as in our workshops, we hope to open up the mysteries and dispel the myths of glass painting. Many people are wary of attempting this craft, as they feel that you need to be an artist to get the best out of it, but this is simply not true. You can be creative with glass painting at any level: you can simply follow a basic pattern or you can create your own freehand masterpieces. This book is designed both for beginners and those who have painted on glass before. All the basic techniques are covered for those of you just starting out and for all those who are already fans of glass painting, we have included many decorative and more advanced techniques, some of which you will certainly not have come across before. Whether you read every page, or dip in when looking for a particular effect, this book will be a great source of reference for everyone involved in this truly absorbing craft

When we sat down to plan the book we were amazed at how many different techniques there were to include. In devising new methods and techniques, we have always been prepared to push back the boundaries; if someone said, don't mix this with that, it won't work, we didn't listen. Most new discoveries are the results of accidents or doing something against the accepted way. Sometimes the consequences of our ideas take us completely by surprise. Don't be afraid to make mistakes and don't be afraid to experiment – you may well come up with new techniques of your own.

In writing this book it was our intention to give you the most comprehensive guide possible to glass painting and we believe that we have achieved that. With over 90 techniques to choose from, you should find everything you need to get the effects you want. The techniques are designed to equip you with the skills and knowledge to get the most from the projects, many of which we have designed especially for this book. All of the techniques and projects are explained and illustrated in an easy to follow, step-by-step format, which makes the book simple to use and will, we hope, encourage you to get the most from your glass painting.

For years we resisted writing this book and giving away our secrets and innovations; we wanted to wait until the time was right and that time is now. So here it is, 20 years of experience, invention and expertise – enjoy it!

Alan. D. Gear

Barry L Freestone

Materials and equipment

The great thing about glass painting is that you don't have to spend too much money to get started. All you need is outliner, glass, paints, a brush, kitchen paper and space on the kitchen table to work in. Many techniques use ordinary household items and you can buy more specialist items as you develop your interest in the craft.

△ **Brushes** From left to right; a very fine No.2 brush for detailed work and flowing paint onto glass; a big, soft brush for thicker paints; a medium-sized brush can be useful; a stippling brush for stencilling; a rubber-tipped brush that is good for glass painting as it does not create any air bubbles and you can also use it to drag patterns into paint.

△ **Knives** From left to right: a craft knife has many uses including cutting out mistakes in outliner or paint and helping lift pipe-and-peel outliner off glass. A heavy-duty retractable craft knife is useful for cutting plastic. (See 63 Working with plastic, page 61.) We use a palette knife a lot to spread gel paints.

Masking tape Use this to stick templates to glass or to mask a pattern to stipple or sponge over.

◁ **Scissors** A medium-sized pair, with sharp blades, is appropriate for most tasks, though you may find a pair of nail scissors useful for tricky jobs.

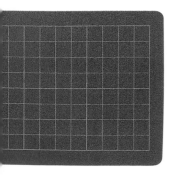

◁ **Cutting mat** Use this to protect your worksurface when cutting out stencils and painted film for mosaics.

◁ **Biscuit cutters** Use these to mark painted glass or to cut shapes out of dry pipe-and-peel paint. (See 85 Creating a stamped effect, page 77 and 89 Using biscuit cutters, page 80.)

△ **Ruler** A steel ruler is best for cutting out stencils. You also use a ruler in tilt painting (See 76 Tilt painting, page 71) and, of course, for measuring.

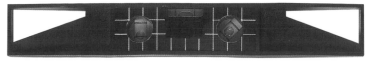

△ **Spirit level** Use this to check that your worksurface is completely level. If it isn't, even by the smallest amount, the paint will flow to one side of the project you are working on.

◁ **Plastic bubble feet**
Stick these to the bottom of glass projects to help protect the surfaces they will stand on.
(See 15 Etched coasters, page 118 and 20 Layered picture frame, page 128.)

◁ **Bradawl**
Use this to make holes in thick film and self-adhesive lead.
(See 2 Celestial mobile, page 90 and 17 Suncatcher, page 122.)

◁ **Tweezers**
Unless you are blessed with slim fingers and steady hands, you will find these useful for embedding an object into paint.
(See 87 Embedding objects in paint, page 78.)

▷ **T-square** A metal t-square is ideal for ensuring lines are straight when cutting glass.
(See 58 Cutting straight lines in glass, page 58.)

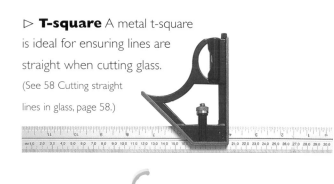

△ **Hot stencil cutter** This is brilliant for cutting stencils out of acetate.
(See 81 Stencilling with brushing paint or outliner, page 75 and 82 Stencilling with gel paint, page 75.)

△ **Plastic food wrap** This is very useful for wrapping over a plate or a palette to keep it clean and it can also be used to stipple paint onto glass with
(See Painting and paints, pages 36-55.)

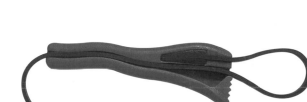

△ **Bottle opener** We find this indispensable for opening bottles of paint, as once the bottle has been used, paint on the rim can seal the bottle tightly.

▷ **Glass bevels**
These come in variety of shapes and sizes. Drill holes in them then paint them and hang them up, or stick them to plain or mirror glass.
(See 65 Using ultra-violet glue, page 62.)

△ **Cocktail sticks and cotton buds**
These have so many uses, from smoothing paint and popping air bubbles to mark-making.
(See 41 Pipe-and-peel paints, page 46 and 79 Using a turntable, page 72.)

Greaseproof paper This is a very important piece of equipment; outlining bags are made from it.

(See 1 How to make an outlining bag, page 17.)

▷▽ Gold outliner

This, and silver outliner, is commonly available in either a bottle or a tube. Bottles are usually more economical and the outliner can be decanted into outlining bags for use.

(See 2 How to outline, page 19.)

▷ Black outliner This

is usually available in bottles of different sizes. You can pipe straight from the smallest bottle, but it is more economical, and to our minds, easier, to buy a large bottle and fill outlining bags from it.

(See 2 How to outline, page 19.)

△ Oven-bake outliner

These can be used straight from the tube as the long, thin nozzle is ideal for outlining.

(See 6 Oven-bake outliner, page 21.)

△ **Boning tool** This is used to press the lead flat to the glass and nip in the joins.

(21 See Using self-adhesive lead, page 32.)

◁▽ **Rubber stamp and ink pad** As long as you choose a permanent ink, you can stamp designs onto glass and then paint them with glass paints. (See 17 Stamping an outline, page 28.)

◁ Self-adhesive lead and copper foil

From left to right; 6mm- (¼in-) wide oval-profiled, brass-coloured lead; 3mm- (⅛in-) wide split lead; copper foil; 9mm- (⅜in-) wide antique-effect lead; 9mm- (⅜in-) wide flat lead; 6mm- (¼in-) wide oval-profiled lead. This is only a selection of the colours and widths available. Self-adhesive lead and copper foil can be used to make outlines and edge projects, and the flat lead is used in making suncatchers.

(See 21 Using self-adhesive lead, page 32 and 17 Suncatcher, page 122.)

◁ **Pens** From left to right: gold and silver pens; coloured felt tipped pens; professional drawing pens. These can be used both to outline designs and to colour them instead of paints. Choose pens with permanent ink so that the finished work won't smudge.

(See 20 Penning an outline, page 31.)

◁ Solvent-based pearl paints
These are opaque with a pearlised finish when dry and are available in a range of colours. (See 37 Solvent-based pearl paints, page 42.)

◁ Iridescent paints
These change colour subtly as the light reflects off them.
(See 50 Iridescent paints, page 52.)

△ Solvent-based transparent paints
These are the most commonly used type of glass paints and many brands are available in a wide range of colours.
(See 38 Solvent-based transparent paints, page 43.)

△ Water-based paints
Some brands of these are child-safe, but do check the label before allowing children to paint with them.
(See 40 Water-based paints, page 45.)

△ Oven-bake paints
As the name suggests, these paints can be baked in the oven and are then more or less permanent.
(See 42 Oven-bake paints, page 47.)

△ Light bulb paints
These are specially made to resist the heat given off by a light bulb and are available in a range of colours.
(See 44 Light bulb paints, page 49.)

◁ Pipe-and-peel paints
These come in a variety of styles of bottle, most of which allow you to use the paint straight from them
(See 41 Pipe-and-peel paints, page 46.)

◁▽ Air-drying polyester-based surface conditioner and paints
You must brush the surface conditioner onto the glass before painting it or the paint will not adhere properly. These paints are more-or less permanent when dry.
(See 43 Air-drying polyester-based paints, page 48.)

△ Gel paints
These are thick and give a textured effect on glass.
(See 39 Gel paints, page 44.)

▷ Hobby enamel paints
These are usually available in small tins that contain just the right amount of paint for most glass painting projects.
(See 52 Hobby enamel paints, page 54.)

▽ ▷ Frosting cream, spray and varnish

These are either brushed or sprayed onto glass to create a frosted finish.

(See 47 Frosting paints, page 51.)

△ Metallic paints and creams

Gold, or silver or copper, paint (left) and gilt cream (right) can be used to add touches of sparkle to projects or to colour dry outliner.

(See 51 Metallic paints, page 52.)

△ Thinners
Different types of paints have different bases that will require different thinners. Check the labels and always use the right type of thinners for the paint you are using.

◁ Artist's acrylic paints

These are available in a wide range of colours and finishes. They come in either bottles (shown) or tubes.

(See 49 Artist's acrylic paints, page 52.)

△ Aluminium foil
Put this on the back of painted glass to help reflect the light back into the painted design.

(See 90 Using aluminium foil, page 81.)

△ Luminous paints

These come in a variety of colours and styles of container.

(See 46 Luminous paints, page 50.)

◁ Varnish
This can be useful as a protective layer over some types of paint.

(See 64 Using varnishes, page 61.)

◁ △ Etching cream
This comes in assorted containers and can be pink, purple, blue or white in colour. Always read the manufacturer's instructions carefully before using it.

(See Etching, pages 66-68.)

◁ Household emulsion paints

These can be bought in sample pots (shown), which are the perfect size for most glass painting projects.

(See 53 Household emulsion paints, page 54.)

◁ Household gloss paints

These are available in a wide range of colours and we suggest that you buy the smallest available tin.

(See 54 Household gloss paints, page 55.)

◁ Metal leaf
From left to right: gold, multi-metal, silver, copper. This works very well in conjunction with glass painting and can give a project a really rich look.

(See 92 Using metal leaf, page 82.)

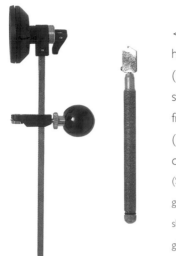

◁ Glass cutters A hand-held glass cutter, (right) is used for cutting straight lines and shapes from glass. A circle cutter (left) is, of course, used for cutting circles.

(See 58 Cutting straight lines in glass, page 58, 61 Cutting glass shapes, page 60 and 60 Cutting glass circles, page 59.)

△ Bottle cutter

This may look rather odd, but it is in fact a tool for cutting the tops off glass bottles.

(See 59 Cutting glass bottles, page 58.)

△ Heavy gloves

Use these to protect your hands when handling freshly cut glass.

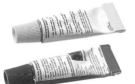

△ Silicone glue This is available in small tubes but it is much more economical to buy it in large dispensers and decant it into an outlining bag for use.

(See 67 Using silicone glue, page 63.)

△ Ultra-violet glue

This needs either light from an ultra-violet lamp or direct sunlight to cure it.

(See 65 Using ultra-violet glue, page 62.)

△ Safety glasses Always wear these to protect your eyes when cutting glass, as sharp chips can fly off the main piece of glass while you are cutting it.

△ Epoxy glue A two-part glue that works well on painted and unpainted glass. Choose a fast-drying kind.

(See 66 Using epoxy glue, page 62.)

△ Sponges and scouring pads These can be used to sponge paint onto glass or to create textures.

(See 14 Sponging with outliner, page 27 and 85 Creating a stamped effect, page 77.)

△ Rubber gloves You should wear these when using etching cream or uncoated lead. They are also useful if you have an allergy to any of the paints. We find these thin gloves the easiest to work in, and they can be thrown away after use.

(See Etching, pages 66-68.)

△ Moulds These come in an enormous number of shapes and sizes and are best used with pipe-and-peel paints.

(See 91 Using moulds, page 81.)

△ Glass sanding pad

Use this to take the sharp edges off cut-out pieces of glass.

(See 58 Cutting straight lines in glass, page 58.)

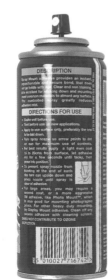

◁ Spray glue

Spray this onto the back of a stencil to hold it in place on the glass. (See 81 Stencilling with brushing paint or outliner, page 75 and 82 Stencilling with gel paint, page 75.)

techniques

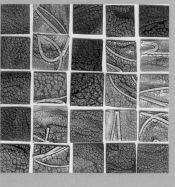

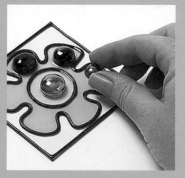

We have always tried to think of new ways of using basic paints and outliners and have developed a lot of the decorative techniques shown in this part of the book over the years that we have been painting glass. Some techniques came about as the result of an accident, others by design; some are adapted from methods used in other crafts or professions.

We have also looked at ways of making jobs easier and more efficient to do. For instance, we have developed a range of films that can be painted onto, which makes awkward shapes much easier to paint. Some people think that making things easier is a little like cheating, but we believe that if a new technique or product works well, then why not use it. Some of our short cuts have been developed as a result of having to make things more quickly for our retail business – they worked for us, they should work for you.

The techniques are grouped into sections, starting with outlining, the most basic technique of all. However, within this section, and within all the other sections, there are some ideas that even experienced glass painters might find new and interesting. We have included techniques unique to ourselves, so do read through all the sections, even if you think at first that they don't hold anything for you.

outlining

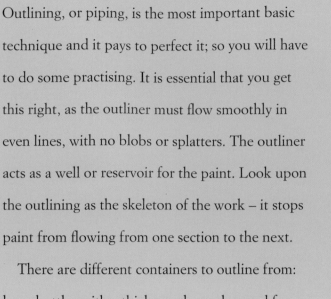

Outlining, or piping, is the most important basic technique and it pays to perfect it; so you will have to do some practising. It is essential that you get this right, as the outliner must flow smoothly in even lines, with no blobs or splatters. The outliner acts as a well or reservoir for the paint. Look upon the outlining as the skeleton of the work – it stops paint from flowing from one section to the next.

There are different containers to outline from: large bottles with a thick nozzle can be used for heavy lines on large items such as windows. Medium-sized bottles are a bit easier to use and give a thinner line. Small bottles are best for fine lines. Outliner also comes in metal tubes and you can outline straight from these. Roll them up from the bottom like a toothpaste tube, but make sure the cap is on when doing this, or you may give the ceiling a makeover. 'That's very artistic,' was Barry's comment when Alan made this mistake. However, we always make our own outlining bags and we recommend that you do as well, as we think that they are easier and more economical to use than commercially available containers.

Many outliners have different properties. Some are made to adhere to glass very well and others are designed to peel off so that you can move the designs around. So, do choose the right outliner for each project. If you use a peel-off outliner on a window prone to condensation, don't be surprised if it is all lying on the windowsill one morning.

1 How to make an outlining bag

In our opinion a most important piece of equipment for any glass painter is a triangle of greaseproof paper. This can be made into an outlining bag, which can be filled with outliner, paint or glue, and is easy to use. It is also cost effective, as you can buy larger bottles of a product, which often work out cheaper than smaller ones, and fill your bags from them. Also, if you don't use all the contents of an outlining bag, you can squeeze them back into the bottle to be used again.

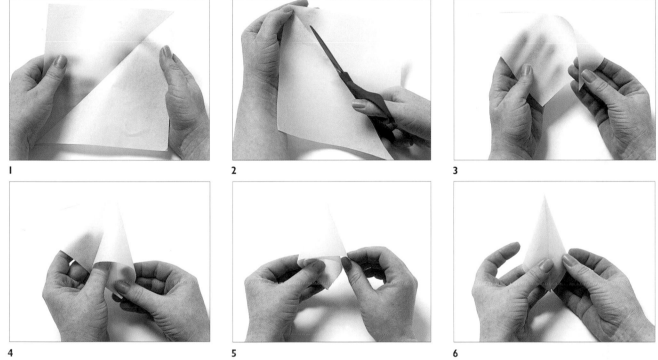

1

2

3

4

5

6

7

8

1 Cut a square of good-quality greaseproof paper; a cheap paper will quickly go soggy and the contents will burst out. We usually cut a 20cm (8in) square, which makes an outlining bag that is perfect for doing fairly fine lines. Fold the square in half diagonally.

2 Cut along the folded line to give you two triangles.

3 Take one triangle and, with the point towards you, you curl one corner over so that it meets the centre point.

4 This will form a cone shape. Hold the points together at the bottom.

5 Now take the other corner over the top of the cone and round to the back, making a double-skinned cone.

6 This picture shows you the back of the cone, so that you can see how all the points should line up. However, you don't need to actually turn it round at this stage.

7 With your thumbs on the inside of the cone, push the paper downwards and inwards. At the same time, your fingers, on the outside of the bag, must push the outside flap backwards and outwards. These motions should make a very tight tip at the end of the cone, which is essential or when it is full, the contents will leak out.

8 When the tip of the cone is very tight, hold the paper firmly and fold the points at the open end over once, into the cone.

9

10

11

12

13

14

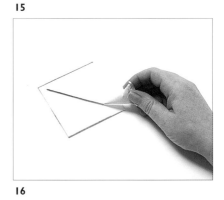

15

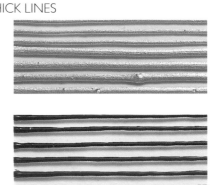

16

9 Now fold them over once again, to stop the bag unfurling.

10 Fill the cone halfway up with your chosen contents. Do not over-fill it or it will be difficult to close up and the contents will ooze out.

11 Fold in one of the corners at an angle, as shown.

12 Fold in the other corner at a corresponding angle.

13 Now fold the end over several times to make a firmly closed bag.

14 The bag should be fat and firm and, if you have folded it properly, none of the contents will ooze out. If the contents drip out of the tip of the bag, you have not made it tight enough. If the contents ooze out of the folded-up end of the bag, you have overfilled it.

15 Now cut the tip of the bag off with a pair of scissors to make a hole the size you want. It is better to cut a smaller hole first and try it. You can always cut the hole a bit bigger if it is too small.

16 Now the bag is ready to work from. As you use up the contents, fold the end of the bag over further to keep it fat and firm. If the bag becomes soggy, or the tip has dried up after you have left it for a while, snip the end off and just squeeze the contents into another bag.

CHOOSING THE RIGHT SIZE OF OUTLINING BAG

You can make outlining bags to any size you need. If you are outlining a large window with thick lines, you will need a large bag. The smallest one shown here is the size demonstrated in the steps and is great for fine, intricate jobs.

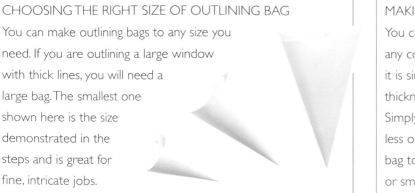

MAKING THIN AND THICK LINES

You can fill a bag with any colour outliner and it is simple to vary the thickness of the lines. Simply cut more or less off the tip of the bag to make a larger or smaller hole.

2 How to outline

Always try to outline towards yourself, the outliner will flow better and you can easily see what you are doing. Work on the area of glass directly in front of you and turn it round as you go – don't lean over areas of wet outliner as you may smudge them. If your hand trembles, support the wrist with your other hand. Keep a piece of kitchen paper to hand to wipe any blobs from the tip of the bag and if outliner gets on your clothes, wash it out immediately.

Because most outliners are water-based, leave them to dry in a warm, dry atmosphere. If the atmosphere is humid, the outliner will absorb the moisture and will go 'all wobbly' (a technical term). Different makes of outliner have different drying times and the thicker the line, the longer the outliner will take to dry. We find it best to leave outliner to dry naturally, but you can speed up the process with a hairdryer, a fan heater or by putting the work in an oven or under a grill on a very low setting. Don't be tempted to turn the oven or grill up high, as if you do the outliner will bubble as the moisture evaporates and leave you with a pitted line.

1   2   3

1 To begin outlining, touch the tip of the outlining bag to the glass where you want the line to start.

2 Squeeze the bag quite firmly and, as the outliner emerges from the bag, lift the tip up, away from the glass. Keep squeezing the bag so that the outliner flows at a smooth rate. Lay the line of outliner down on the glass, keeping the tip of the bag about 1cm (½in)

above the surface. If your outliner breaks in mid-line, touch the tip of the bag to the broken end and continue the line.

3 When you want to finish the line, stop squeezing the bag and touch the tip to the glass where you want the line to stop. To finish the line neatly, lift the tip away from the glass in the direction that the line is travelling.

CLEARING AIR BUBBLES FROM BOTTLES OF OUTLINER

If you are using bottles of outliner, always keep them upside down in a container. This allows the outliner to flow to the nozzle and pushes the air bubbles away from it, so you won't get a 'raspberry' sound as outliner splatters all over your work when you squeeze the bottle.

Always replace the cap when you are not using the bottle to stop the nozzle from becoming blocked with dry outliner. If the nozzle does get blocked, try pushing in a pin, or if it is really hard, leave the nozzle in a glass of water for a short time, then wash it out under a running tap with a paint brush: don''t use your best brush though.

CORRECTING MISTAKES IN OUTLINER

If you make a mistake you can try to wipe it off straightaway. However, we find it more precise, and less messy, to let it dry, then cut the mistake out with a craft knife and re-draw the line with fresh outliner.

3 Using a practice sheet

The usual method of outlining is to place a template of the design you want to use under the glass and then outline over it. Enlarge the Practice Sheet on a photocopier and use it to perfect your outlining technique and to get used to following a template before you start on your first project.

The thinner the glass is, the easier it is to outline over a template beneath it. If you have to use thick 6mm (¼in) glass, because the surface is so far away from the design it can seem as though you have double vision as you try to outline the design. To help counteract this, have the template photocopied in a different colour from the outliner you are using. Black-on-black will send you cross-eyed.

Place an old piece of glass or plastic over the Practice Sheet (see page 165) and, starting with the straight lines, work your way around the page – not just once, but many times. If you are working on glass, either wash off the outliner straight away or leave it to dry and peel it off.

I have found that 99% of our students get the knack of outlining, eventually. It may take an hour, a day or a week, but even if you think you are that 1% that can't get it right, don't give up. If you find that you start to make a lot of mistakes, stop, have a

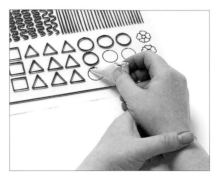

cup of tea or watch some television, and then go back and have another go – it will click in place with practice.

All this practising will actually save you money, and time, in the long run, as you won't have to cut out all the wobbly lines on your project and

redo them. So do be prepared to use up a bottle of outliner in practising. Even when you have been outlining for a while, go back to the Practice Sheet now and again to keep you up to standard.

4 Over-outlining

Outliners are available in an assortment of colours. Black or grey gives a leaded-line effect. Gold, silver, bronze and copper are the colours that we use to finish off projects. It is better not to use these colours as a main outliner, as if you accidentally go over them with a strong paint colour you can see where the mistake has been made, but with black or grey outliner, it doesn't show.

There may be occasions when you want to paint a design freehand, without outlining it first, but you still want the end result to have an outline. To achieve this, simply paint the design onto the glass, let the paint dry, then carefully outline around it.

Outline and paint the design in the usual way (see 2 How to outline, page 19, and Painting and paints, pages 36-55). Wait until the paint is completely dry before you over-outline the design. Simply follow the original outlines with the coloured outliner. Either outline straight from the bottle or use an outlining bag (see 1 How to make an outlining bag, page 17).

5 Under-outlining

This is an excellent technique as it is not only decorative but, as the outlining is on the back of the glass, it also protects your work. Under-outlining is ideal for plates, tables, coasters, table mats or trays, and works really well if you use gold or silver outliner. Do remember that when you turn the glass over you will see the design in reverse, so you may need to reverse the template before you start outlining. We have included a reverse alphabet and numerals in the Motif Library especially for this technique.

1 Outline the design in the usual way and let dry (see 2 How to outline, page 19).
2 Paint over the whole design, completely covering the outliner, or paint in between the lines in the usual way and leave it to dry. (See Painting and paints, pages 36-55.)

△ *When you turn it over the coloured outlining will stand out and look very effective.*

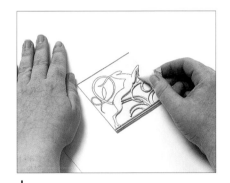

1

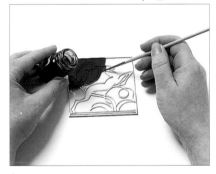

2

6 Oven-bake outliner

These outliners are applied in the same way as normal outliner and can also be sponged and stippled. They are available in a variety of colours and blend well together, so you can create some interesting effects. They have a good resistance to dishwashers and washing-up detergents after they have been baked, and they also work very well on ceramics and metals. You could use them to decorate your knives and forks to match your dinner service.

Follow the manufacturer's instructions for these outliners for the drying and baking times. You must let them dry out completely before you bake them, otherwise the moisture will expand and mark the surface of the outliner. Do not overcook the outliner or bake it at a higher temperature than recommended or it may discolour.

7 Outlining with gel paint

To create coloured outlines, you can use any of the thick glass paints as an outlining medium; gel paint works especially well. You can either outline straight from the paint tube, if it has its own nozzle, or you can fill an outlining bag and outline from that.

When using gel as an outliner a little more care has to be taken, as the line of gel can break easily. You must also let it dry completely before you paint the design, or the paint may dissolve the gel. However, once it is dry you can combine it with any type of glass paint.

OUTLINING FROM THE TUBE
You may get some watery residue coming out of a tube of gel paint when you start outlining. Squeeze this onto kitchen paper towel or hold the tube at the end and give it a good shake, before you start outlining. Always outline onto dry glass, as any moisture will dissolve the gel paint.

8 Pipe-and-peel outlining

▷ Small designs scattered across a vase.

We like using this technique because it makes projects on rounded items, such as bottles and light bulbs, much easier to do. You do the outlining on flat glass and then transfer it to the item you want to paint, which is much easier than outlining onto a curved surface.

This is also a useful technique for larger designs: you can pipe-and-peel a large window in sections and assemble it on the glass like a jigsaw.

There are different makes of outliner on the market; most of them will peel off when dry, but you may need to experiment.

▷ A large design placed centrally on a vase.

Pipe-and-peeling a small design

1 Place the template under a clean piece of glass and outline it in the usual way (see 2 How to outline, page 19).

2 When dry, peel the outlined design off the glass – a craft knife will help you to lift the edge, then you can pull it with your fingers (see inset). Don't worry if it stretches, it will spring back into shape as long as you don't pull too hard.

3 When you have peeled the outlined design off, the back will be slightly tacky and you can simply stick it in position on your glass item.

4 Paint the item in the usual way (see Painting and paints, pages 36-55).

1

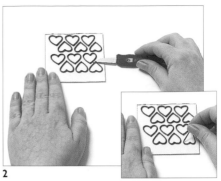

2

3

4

Pipe-and-peeling a large design

1 Outline the design as described above and let it dry. We find it easier to hold the glass upside down when peeling off larger outlined shapes. Slowly peel the design away from the glass, moving the glass around and peeling towards the middle. Be careful not to get the lines tangled up, as if you do it will be almost impossible to separate them again.

2 Lay the design, tacky-side up, on a piece of kitchen paper and leave it for a few minutes. This allows the outliner to spring back into shape if you have stretched it a bit in peeling it off the glass. It also allows it to dry slightly and harden up a little, which makes it easier to handle.

3 You can gently pick up the outlined design and place it onto the glass item. Alternatively, position the glass item over the outlined design lying on the kitchen paper, then press it down onto the outliner. Roll the item from side to side to ensure that the design is stuck firmly on to the glass.

4 Pat the outlined design smooth with your finger and it is ready for painting.

1

2

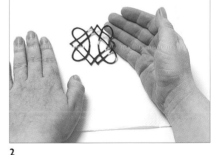

3

4

REPOSITIONING OUTLINED DESIGNS

Early on it is possible to un-peel the outlined design and reposition it. Depending on the outliner you are using, you have between twelve and twenty-four hours before it sets. Once hard it is difficult to move successfully and generally speaking, the longer the outliner is left, the harder it becomes.

9 Transferring designs onto mirror glass

Outlining onto mirror glass presents a problem, as obviously you can't see a template placed underneath it. The answer is to use carbon paper.

1 Place the carbon paper face down onto the mirror. Place design on top, and tape it in position if it has a tendency to slip. Trace over the design with a pen or pencil, pressing down to imprint the lines onto the mirror.

1

2 Peel off the carbon paper to reveal the transferred design.

3 Outline the design in the usual way (see 2 How to outline, page 19). Wipe off any remaining carbon ink with a cloth before you start painting the mirror glass or it will discolour the paints.

2

3

10 Transferring designs onto curved surfaces

This can be difficult to do and you may prefer to use the pipe-and-peel technique. However, if you want to work straight onto curved glass, this is the best way of doing it.

1 Cut out the template closely, cutting vents in between the elements of the pattern as much as possible.

2 Place the template inside the glass item and tape it in position with masking tape, pushing it up against the glass.

3 Use small pieces of masking tape to hold all the template parts position. The cut-out vents will help you push the paper right up to the glass.

4 Outline the design in the usual way (see 2 How to outline, page 19). If it is a large or awkward glass item, you can cushion it on a rolled-up piece of fabric or a towel, or you can use two blocks of wood, or even cut out a section in a cardboard box to support the item. If the design is right around the glass, outline it in sections, letting each section dry before you turn the glass round to do the next one.

1

2

3

4

11 Transferring designs onto narrow vessels

If you want to outline a design straight onto a narrow glass vessel like a bottle, it can be very difficult to get the paper template in and out of it. You could avoid the problem and use the pipe-and-peel technique or you can use the following method.

1 Trim the template as small as possible.
2 Tape a length of wire to the back of the template – florist's wire is ideal.
3 Insert the template into the bottle and, holding the wire, push it up against the glass. You can bend the wire over the neck of the bottle and hang the template in position.

1

2

MARKING A LINE ON A CURVED VESSEL

An easy way to mark a straight, even line all the way around a curved glass vessel is to fill it with water up to where you want the line, then mark the water level with a pen all the way round. If you want to mark another line, either pour off the excess or add more water. Pour out all the water and outline over the pen line.

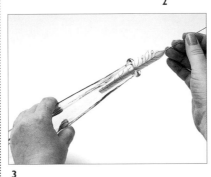

3

4

4 If the template is moving around, pour pulses into the bottle, behind the template, to push it up against the glass and keep it in position.
5 Outline the design in the usual way (see 2 How to outline, page 19). Then, pour the pulses out, let the outliner dry and paint it.

5

12 Embedding into outliner

There are a variety of materials that can be attached to glass, but you don't always have to use glue to stick them on. Instead you can embed straight objects into wet outliner.

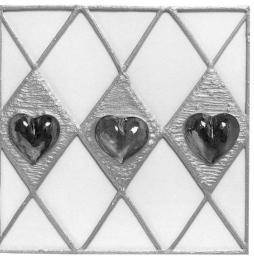

1 Outline a shape large enough to contain the object you want to embed and fill it in with the outliner. You can use any colour of outliner, but the infill should be the same colour as the outline; if you use different colours they will bleed into one another and look messy.
2 Carefully drop the object into it, gently press it down and leave the outliner to dry. If you are embedding a very small object, you may find it easier to hold it with a pair of tweezers rather than in your fingers.

1

2

CHOOSING OBJECTS TO EMBED
Always use objects appropriate in size to your project – small projects are best embedded with small objects. With larger projects you can use a mixture of small and large objects. Experiment with things such as glass shells, shapes, buttons, coins, glass beads, semi precious stones and resin beads that work well on glass.

13 Scratching with outliner

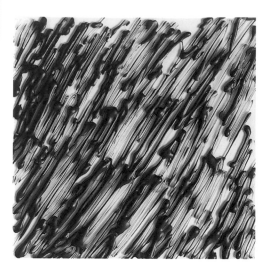

You can scratch outliner onto the glass to create textured and shaded effects which can give depth to your glass painting. Cut a fairly small hole in the tip of the outlining bag, keep the tip on the glass and drag it across the area you want to fill in, using short zigzag strokes. You can add this effect before or after painting the design, depending on how intense you want it to be.

14 Sponging with outliner

There is a vast array of different types of sponges to choose from: natural, synthetic, pre-cut shapes or just salvaged pieces of furnishing foam. You can use the sponge just as you buy it with a close texture, which will give you a uniform effect. Or rip and cut bits out of the sponge to give you a coarser texture. You can sponge with outliner or thick paint. You can also use a sponge to stencil designs – gold and silver outliner looks very effective stencilled on glass – and if you wish to cover large areas of glass, the sponged effect on its own looks very good.

△ *Black outliner.*

△ *Gold outliner.*

△ *Silver outliner.*

△ *Gold and silver outliner combined.*

15 Stippling with outliner

This technique is very similar to sponging, but instead of a sponge you use a stippling brush to put the outliner or thick paint onto the glass.

Squeeze some outliner onto a covered plate. Dab your sponge onto the outliner and take off any excess by dabbing it onto the plate. Then just press it onto the glass as thinly or thickly as you want.

You can sponge onto glass with any colour outliner: gold looks good around a glass plate for instance, or sponge silver onto the back of a glass plate and paint over it or dip it. These techniques are simple but can look stunning.

KEEPING A PLATE CLEAN

Cover a plate with plastic food wrap and squeeze the outliner onto that. Then, when you have finished sponging, just throw away the wrap – this keeps your plates nice and clean.

Squeeze the outliner onto a covered plate and dab the brush into it. Dab the excess outliner off onto the plate, then stipple outliner onto the glass as thickly or as thinly as you want. The stippling brush must always be held in an upright position.

16 Silhouetting with outliner

We use this technique when we want a strongly outlined design; it works especially well on mirrors. You need to use an outliner that will peel off easily.

1 Using a palette knife, spread outliner all over the area of plain glass or mirror glass you wish to cover and leave it to dry.

2 Place a piece of carbon paper face down onto the outliner and lay the template on top of it. Trace over the template with a pencil, then remove both it and the carbon paper.

3 On the sections you want to remove, cut along the transferred lines with a craft knife, making sure you cut right through the outliner.

4 Peel the outliner away, keeping the knife handy to lift the edges and to cut any little bits you may have missed.

5 Paint the glass from the front or the back (see Painting and paints, pages 36-55).

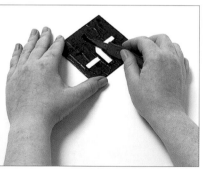

1

2

3

4

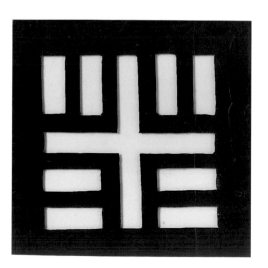

5

17 Stamping an outline

Stamping is another way to get an outlined effect and there are a multitude of stamps on the market. You need a stamping pad with ink that will adhere well to glass and not smudge. Ask your retailer for the right kind.

18 Pre-cut vinyl outlines

There are literally thousands of pre-cut vinyl outlines that can be used with glass paints. Some people say it's cheating, but we say, if you want to use them, why not.

You can just peel them off, stick them onto the glass and use them instead of outliner. They can be painted from the front or the back. With gold and silver outlines you have to be more careful if you paint from the front, as the paint will show if you get it on the vinyl.

1

2

3

1 Press the stamp onto the ink pad and then press it squarely and firmly onto the glass.

2 Lift the stamp cleanly off the glass. You may need a few goes to produce a perfect image, as the stamps do have a tendency to slip on the glass and smudge the design.

However, if you make a mistake, wash the ink off, dry the glass thoroughly and have another go.

3 You must let the ink dry completely before you start to paint (see Painting and paints, pages 36-55).

◁ *You can also stamp onto painted glass with water-based outliner. Squeeze some outliner out and spread it thinly. Press the stamp into it, dab the excess onto a paper towel then stamp onto your glass. This works well with gold and silver outliner.*

CLEANING A STAMP

If you have used outliner, wash it off as soon as you have used the stamp – a toothbrush will help to scrub it clean. If you don't do this, the outliner will dry and clog up all the fine detail in the stamp.

---

1 Peel the vinyl outline off the backing sheet.

2 Stick it to the glass.

3 Paint it in the usual way (see Painting and paints, pages 36-55).

1

2

3

◁ *Gold, silver and black outlines can be stuck directly onto painted glass to create a filigree-style design.*

◁ *Vinyl letters or numerals can be added to birthday cards or to clocks.*

19 Photocopying an outline

You can buy acetate film that can be run through a photocopier. It is often used in projectors, but you can also paint onto it. This film is great if you want to incorporate intricate designs, black and white photographs or text into your work. To make greetings cards, which are now available with pre-cut apertures, paint a suitable design onto film, cut it out and glue it into the card. You can just paint photocopies, or you can outline the main areas of the design with ordinary outliner. A self-adhesive film that you can put through a photocopier is also available.

1

2

3

△ A painted photocopy.

△ An outlined and painted photocopy.

1 Photocopy the design onto film.

2 Carefully paint the photocopied design (see Painting and paints, pages 36-55).

3 Alternatively, you can also outline the main areas of the design in the usual way (see 2 How to outline, page 19), then paint the outlined areas, carefully going over the photocopied lines within them. You must be cautious because if you brush too hard, you may disturb the toner and smudge it.

CHOOSING THE RIGHT PAINT

When painting on film, choose a glass paint that stays malleable when dry, so that if the film is bent the paint will not crack and flake off. Check with the manufacturer that the paint you want to use is suitable.

PAINTING A LARGE AREA

When painting a large area of a design, if you go all the way around in one direction, by the time you get back to the beginning the paint will be drying and you will get a blemish line. To counteract this, paint in one direction for a short distance and then the other direction, also for a short distance. Keep going backwards and forwards until both ends meet and you will get a smooth join.

20 Penning an outline

Pens can be used to create an outlined effect, you simply draw onto the glass. There are many pens to choose from; felt tips, technical pens, waterproof pens, etc. So be sure to choose the right pen for the type of paint you are using. We find it best to let the ink dry on the glass before you attempt to paint. There are also many thicknesses of pens and, with the right ink, you can incorporate some intricate filigree effects into your work.

△ Paint the piece carefully because there are no raised outlines to keep the paint in place. However, even with the most fluid paint, the surface tension will stop it from running over your lines, if you are cautious.

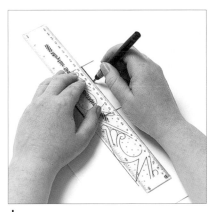

1

1 If you want to draw a straight line, use a ruler, but turn it over so the ink does not run down the side of the ruler and smudge.

2 Use a fine pen for thinner lines and small details.

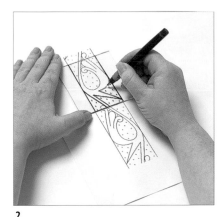

2

◁ Pens are also good for adding detail to finished painted glass. For instance, fine details on a face or veins on a leaf.

Adding colour with pens

You can also use pens to add coloured detail to painted glass; indeed you can use them instead of paint.

1 Lay a design under a piece of glass and, using waterproof pens, colour it in.

2 Once you have completed the colouring, use a fine black pen to outline the design.

1

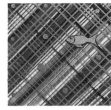

2

◁ This leaf design was drawn onto blue painted glass with gold and silver pens.

◁ Red and black pens on yellow painted glass were used to make this design.

◁ The drawn lines of this grid pattern, with gold dots and a little fish added, almost completely obscure the original painted glass.

21 Using self-adhesive lead

If you want to give your project a more traditional look, use self-adhesive lead as an outliner. The lead comes with a backing paper that you peel off and then you can stick the lead straight onto the glass. The lead we used for the following techniques is specially coated to prevent you getting lead on your skin. But if you are unsure whether the lead you are using is coated, always wear rubber gloves when using it. After handling any type of lead, wash your hands before touching food or smoking.

The intricacy of the design you choose determines the thickness of the lead you use: the more complex the design, the thinner the lead strip. There are various ways of applying self-adhesive lead – this is our way of doing it.

1 Clean the glass with a glass cleaner, but not a silicone-based one, as this will prevent the lead from sticking to the glass. Dry the glass with a lint free cloth. Cut the lengths of lead with scissors. It is soft and will cut easily, but don't use your best scissors. The lead has a backing paper that you just peel off as you go along.

2 The 3mm- (⅛in-) wide lead is usually available as a 6mm- (¼in-) wide strip that is split down the middle – just pull it in half.

3 Lay the template under the piece of glass. Start by sticking down the shortest lengths on the design, but cut the lengths of lead slightly longer than you need, so you have something to hold to help you position the lengths. Cutting lead to length before sticking it down is easier than trying to work from the roll.

4 Complete all the shortest sections of the design then move on to the next longest sections. The longer lengths lie over the ends of the shorter lengths to give a neat finish.

1

2

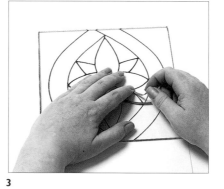

3

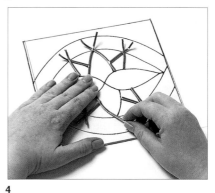

4

WORKING WITH LEAD
Always keep the lead at an ambient temperature. If the lead is cold it is harder to work with. Don't work on damp glass or in a humid atmosphere as it will be harder to stick the lead to the glass.

STICKING DOWN LONG LENGTHS OF LEAD
Before you start sticking the longer lengths down, give the lead a little tug – it stretches it slightly and this seems to make it bend more easily.

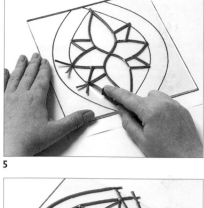

5

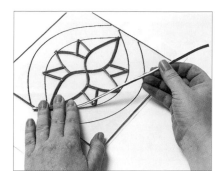

8

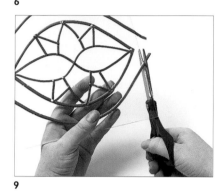

9

10

5 Trim off any protruding ends of lead with a craft knife.

6 On the longer sections of the design you can use a wider gauge lead. Hold it at one end and, with the other hand, press it onto the glass.

7 Press the lead down along all the lengths with a hard rubber roller or the flat end of a boning tool.

A boning tool is plastic tool you can buy with the lead that helps you flatten it and seal the joins. If you don't have a boning tool, an old wooden clothes peg or a length of doweling will do.

8 Next, with the pointed end of the boning tool, push in the lead where it runs over another strip. Push hard so that the overlying piece of lead is tight up against the piece underneath. This seals the joins, so that when you paint the design the paint will not run under the lead into an adjacent section. You can use the back of a knife to do this, though ideally you shouldn't use metal tools as they can mark the lead.

9 Trim off any ends of lead protruding beyond the glass with scissors.

10 When you have leaded your glass, you can always add some extra detail with outliner (see 2 How to outline, page 19). Leave it to dry then paint the whole item in the usual way (see Painting and paints, pages 36–55).

REMOVING PAINT FROM LEAD

If you get some paint on the lead, don't try to wipe it off. Let it dry completely, then gently scrape it off with a craft knife.

MAKING TIGHT CURVES

If your design demands tight curves, hold one end of the lead down firmly and pull it hard around the curve, pressing it down as you go.

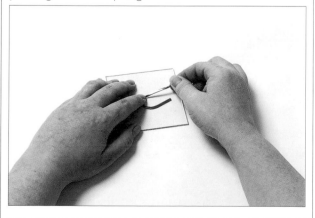

OUTLINING   **33**

22 Using self-adhesive film to colour leaded designs

Film offers another way of adding colour to a leaded design. You can either use it as we have here, or stick the film to the glass and then stick the lead over it.

1 Either buy coloured self-adhesive film, or paint clear film the day before you want to use it, to give it plenty of time to dry.

2 Cut out a piece of film just large enough to cover the section of the design you are working on.

3 Remove the film's backing sheet to expose the adhesive side and lay the film in place.

4 Using a boning tool, push the film up to and into the corners of the lead, pressing down to make sure that it sticks firmly to the glass.

5 With a craft knife, cut the film along the inner edge of the leaded section.

6 Peel off the excess film.

5

2

3

4

6

23 Using self-adhesive lead to hold glass to glass

You can fix painted glass to windows with self-adhesive lead. If you put the painted side up to the window, it will seal it in and protect your work.

24 Using self-adhesive copper foil

Traditionally copper foil is used when soldering pieces of glass together. However, you can stick foil onto glass and paint up to it. You can also stick it onto already-painted glass. You can patina the foil to give it an antique look, but make sure that the patina does not react with the paint.

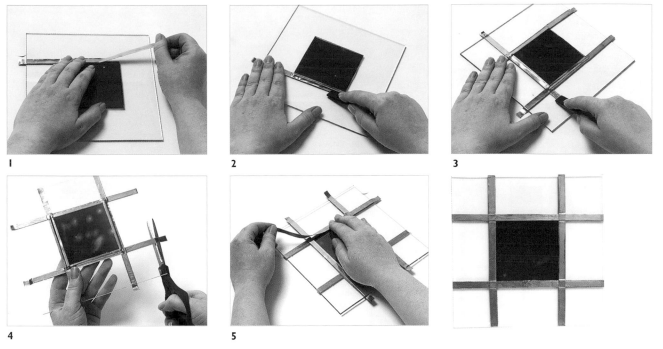

1 Place the painted glass, paint side down, onto clean, clear glass. Stick down 9mm- (⅜in-) wide lead strip, slightly overlapping the edge of the painted glass.

2 Using a boning tool, gently press the lead down on the top and sides of the glass.

3 Continue to stick and press down lengths of lead, overlapping the edge of the painted glass with each one.

4 Cut off any protruding ends.

5 Turn the glass over (or if you are doing a window, go round to the other side) and lead the back of the glass. Stick the strips exactly on top of those on the other side and press them down with the boning tool.

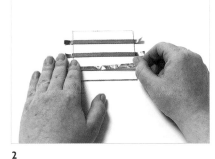

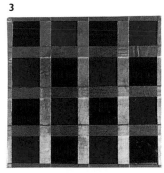

1 Peel the backing off the copper foil.

2 Stick it down on glass.

3 Trim off any protruding ends with sharp scissors.

4 Wrap a strip evenly over each edge of the glass, then trim off the corners.

5 Paint the design from the back, allowing the paint to go over the edge of the foil lines a little so that you get a neat finish on the front (see Painting and paints, pages 36-55).

◁ *When sticking foil onto painted glass, ensure that the paint is fully dry or you may damage it if you lift the foil to reposition it.*

painting
and paints

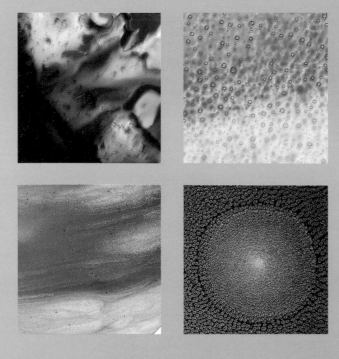

This chapter is divided into two sections: the first section deals with the different methods of applying paint to glass and the second section looks at the different types of paint you can use.

There is a vast array of specially made glass paints and they are all fairly good. We have demonstrated and discussed the most widely used types and they are all paints that we have used ourselves. This section has been a little difficult to put together, as different manufacturers often have slightly different recipes for the same type of paint. This may effect the way you use the paint, so always check the individual manufacturer's instructions.

You will also find that different types of paint have different drying times. The thicker the paint, the longer the drying time. Some paints will be touch-dry in a short time, but will still be soft underneath and can mark easily, so leave them a few days to dry out and go completely hard. There are other paints that can take up to a week to dry. Again, it is always a good idea to check instructions for drying times before you begin a project.

You should always clean glass before you paint it, as dirt or grease can stop the paint from properly adhering to it. There are various brands of glass cleaner on the market, but do test them first to ensure that they don't react with the paint you are using. The way we clean glass is to wash it in very hot water with a few drops of detergent. We leave it on a draining rack and it dries very quickly.

25 Before you start

Cover your worksurface with newspaper; from experience we know you will knock over at least one bottle of paint. Wear old clothes when painting, especially if you are a beginner, and roll up shirt and blouse cuffs – they are always the first things to go into the paint.

Place a piece of white paper under your work before you start painting. It will help you see bits you have missed, as will picking up your work from time to time.

Plan how and what to paint first. We tend to paint all the large areas and the darkest colours first. It is easier to get a drop of yellow out of red paint if you drop some than it is the other way around. If you drop any paint onto another painted area and it leaves a mess when you are trying to clean it up, flood a few drops of clear paint onto the area – it will dissolve the mess and make it easier to clean up. If you drop some unwanted paint onto an unpainted section of glass, it is less messy to let it dry and then scrape it away with a craft knife afterwards.

We tend to paint projects in sections. The outliner acts as a wall, but if you paint immediately adjoining sections one after the other, the paint may bleed across from one to another. Always paint right up to the outliner. Don't be afraid – the surface tension of the paint will stop it flowing over the outline. If you paint over the outliner, however, it may lift as the paint dries. If this happens, just cut across the outliner with a scalpel while the paint is still wet, pull it straight back into position, then cut off any excess.

Always work with the area you wish to paint directly in front of you and move the glass around as you paint. Don't be tempted to lean over a painted area – you will only get paint on the back of your hand or up your arm. Always paint the easy way.

You may trap air bubbles in your brush when you first put it into the paint. Always make sure your brush is well-saturated with paint – the more you dip the brush in, the less bubbles you will get. Keep a folded piece of kitchen paper next to where you work to wipe any bubbles off the tip of your brush.

Always hold the bottle of paint over the area that you are painting, so that the paint can be taken straight down onto the glass. If you leave the paint bottle on the table and try to take the paint across to the glass on your brush, it will drip everywhere.

Beware of red paint; we have found it is always the worst colour to clean up and if it drips into another colour it will stain it badly.

Don't smoke when painting, especially if you are using paints with odours. You don't want to be sucking those fumes into your lungs as well as the smoke, and you don't want ash dropping onto your newly painted glass either. If you are in a dusty space and your work is small enough, put a cardboard box over the top of it to protect it as it dries.

26 Using a fine brush

The majority of our work is done on small areas of glass so we tend to use a No 2 sable brush most of the time. It holds a lot of paint and has a nicely pointed tip for painting fine details.

To flood areas of glass with flowing, solvent paints, make sure that you really saturate the brush with paint – this helps eliminate any air bubbles – then just drop paint onto the glass. Your brush should not touch the glass itself, as this will encourage unwanted air bubbles. Just use the very tip of the brush to flood the paint right up to the outliner or edge of the glass. You will usually find that you need more paint than you thought to achieve a smooth surface. Hold the bottle of paint over the area you are painting so any drips just land on the painted glass.

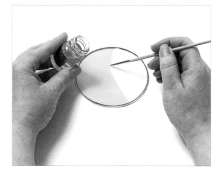

A No. 2 sable brush is not only good for flooding areas of glass with flowing paints, we use it with all the different types of paint for doing fine detailed work as well. To paint details, simply dip the brush into the paint and work directly onto the glass. Do not saturate the brush or the paint will flow everywhere.

The best way to clean this kind of brush is to force all the paint out of the brush by folding a piece of kitchen paper around the bristles and squeezing it down towards the tip of the brush. The brush will stiffen a little overnight, but just flick it and it will become soft again.

RECOMMENDED PAINTS

37 Solvent-based pearl paints, page 42

38 Solvent-based transparent paints, page 43

40 Water-based paints, page 45

42 Oven-bake paints, page 47

43 Air-drying polyester-based paints, page 48

44 Light bulb paints, page 49

46 Luminous paints, page 50

47 Frosting paints, page 51

48 Acrylic glass paints, page 51

49 Artist's acrylic paints, page 52

50 Iridescent paints, page 52

51 Metallic paints, page 52

RECOMMENDED GLASS

All glass surfaces

27 Using a thick brush

Between a No 2 brush and a 2.5cm- (1in-) thick brush there are a variety of thicknesses of brushes that you can use, but we tend to go from one extreme to the other.

A thick brush is especially good when you want to cover a large area of glass. We find that the better the quality and softer the bristles, the less brush strokes you see on the glass and the smoother a surface you get. Simply dip the end of the brush into the paint and brush it onto the glass with long, smooth strokes. Use a stiff-bristled brush if you want to create a more textured effect.

If you are using a water-based paint, then you can just wash out your brush under the tap. If you are

using a solvent-based paint, however, then you must clean the brush with thinners.

RECOMMENDED PAINTS

42 Oven-bake paints, page 47

43 Air-drying polyester-based paints, page 48

45 Brushing paints, page 50

49 Artist's acrylic paints, page 52

51 Metallic paints, page 52

RECOMMENDED GLASS

All glass surfaces

28 Using a stippling brush

As its name suggests, this is a brush for stippling paint onto glass to give a speckled effect. Stippling is a good way of combining different colours of paint, creating a subtle, graduated effect.

Dip the very tip of the bristles into the paint and, holding the brush upright, stipple the paint onto the glass with short, stabbing motions.

If you are using a water-based paint then you can just wash out your brush under the tap. If you are using a solvent-based paint, however, then you must clean the brush with thinners.

RECOMMENDED PAINTS

42 Oven-bake paints, page 47

43 Air-drying polyester-based paints, page 48

44 Light bulb paints, page 49

45 Brushing paints, page 50

46 Luminous paints, page 50

47 Frosting paints, page 51

48 Acrylic glass paints, page 51

49 Artist's acrylic paints, page 52

51 Metallic paints, page 52

RECOMMENDED GLASS

Flat or curved glass surfaces

29 Using pipettes

These are best used with flowing paints and they are useful if you have to cover a large area of glass with paint.

Squeeze the air out of the bulb end of the pipette. Put the open end into the paint, let the bulb go and the pipette will fill up with paint. Then just squeeze the bulb to flow the paint onto the glass. However, if pipettes are not used properly, they will blow lots of bubbles into your paint and you will spend a lot of time getting them out again.

Pipettes can be washed out with water or thinners, but it is quite tricky to get them clean. We tend to use the disposable kind and throw them away after use.

RECOMMENDED PAINTS

37 Solvent-based pearl paints, page 42

38 Solvent-based transparent paints, page 43

40 Water-based paints, page 45

47 Frosting paints, page 51

50 Iridescent paints, page 52

RECOMMENDED GLASS

Flat glass surfaces

30 Using your fingers

This is definitely one of our favourite ways to apply paint and is most effective with thick or gel paints. Some paints may stain your fingers for a few days, so it is best not to use this technique before a dinner party.

Squeeze the paint straight onto the glass and spread it out with your fingers – you can even make patterns and hand prints. Make sure you are not allergic to the paint before you start and only use the water-based paints. If you wish you can wear a rubber glove, but then it is not as much fun.

Remember to wash your hands thoroughly when you have finished painting.

RECOMMENDED PAINTS

39 Gel paints, page 44

41 Pipe-and-peel paints, page 46

51 Metallic paints, page 52

RECOMMENDED GLASS

All glass surfaces

31 Using a sponge

You can sponge paint onto glass with any type of sponge – they can all give different effects. You can also use sponge shapes such as dolphins or flowers.

Put some paint onto a plate then dab the sponge into it. Dab off any excess paint onto kitchen paper, then sponge  straight onto the glass. Sponging works best with the thicker paints. Build up as many layers as you want, mixing different colours together if you wish. This technique is a good one for covering large areas of glass with colour.

Sponging works well with water-based paints, as you can just wash the paint out and use the sponge again. It is much harder to clean solvent-based paints out of sponges, so we tend to just throw them away after using these paints.

RECOMMENDED PAINTS

42 Oven-bake paints, page 47

43 Air-drying polyester-based paints, page 48

44 Light bulb paints, page 49

45 Brushing paints, page 50

46 Luminous paints, page 50

47 Frosting paints, page 51

48 Acrylic glass paints, page 51

49 Artist's acrylic paints, page 52

51 Metallic paints, page 52

RECOMMENDED GLASS

All glass surfaces

32 Using plastic wrap

You must first make sure that the paint does not react with the plastic, but other than that you can use any sort of thin plastic – even plastic bags.

Screw up the plastic into a tight or loose ball and dab it  into paint. Dab off any excess on kitchen paper, then dab paint onto the glass. This technique is good for building up layers of colour and covering large areas of glass.

One of the other good things about this technique is that there is no clearing up; simply throw the plastic away.

RECOMMENDED PAINTS

42 Oven-bake paints, page 47

44 Light bulb paints, page 49

45 Brushing paints, page 50

46 Luminous paints, page 50

47 Frosting paints, page 51

48 Acrylic glass paints, page 51

49 Artist's acrylic paints, page 52

51 Metallic paints, page 52

RECOMMENDED GLASS

All glass surfaces

33 Piping from the bottle

The thick water-based pipe-and-peel paints come in soft plastic bottles that have a fine nozzle at the end that you can pipe from.

Just doodle the paint straight onto the glass. The more roughly you doodle, the more textured the paint looks when it dries. For a smoother finish, go backwards and forwards throughout the paint with a cocktail stick – this breaks it down and the paint lies flatter on the glass. It also gets rid of any bubbles in the paint.

If the nozzle clogs up, pull off the end and scoop out the offending bit of dried paint with a cocktail stick.

RECOMMENDED PAINTS

41 Pipe-and-peel paints, page 46

RECOMMENDED GLASS

All glass surfaces

34 Using a palette knife or spatula

Put the palette knife into a jug of hot water just before you want to use it. Wipe the water off and the heat will help you achieve a smoother finish when spreading the paint.

We mainly use a palette knife with gel paints, which are very thick. Squeeze the paint out of the tube straight onto the glass and then spread it over the surface with the knife. You can mix different colours together in this way. Use the knife to create interesting textures or you can smooth out the gel completely to get a flat finish.

Simply wipe or wash the knife clean after use.

RECOMMENDED PAINTS

39 Gel paints, page 44

RECOMMENDED GLASS

Flat or curved glass surfaces

35 Using an outlining bag

Make up an outlining bag and fill it with thick paint or gel paint, then just pipe straight from it, as you would when outlining.

You can create some interesting effects by layering different colours of gel paint. This piping technique is also useful for applying fine detail to painted glass.

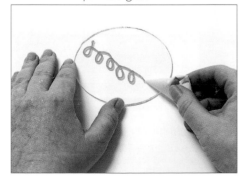

When you have finished piping, squeeze any left-over paint back into its bottle and throw the outlining bag away.

RECOMMENDED PAINTS

39 Gel paints, page 44

43 Air-drying polyester-based paints, page 48

RECOMMENDED GLASS

Flat or curved glass surfaces

36 Using gel paints from the tube

Thick gel paints are sold in soft containers, from which you can squeeze the paint directly onto the glass.

Just squeeze paint all over the glass for a highly textured effect. You may find it necessary to smooth the paint a little with a palette knife. Some gel tubes come with shaped nozzles, a bit like icing nozzles, which give different effects.

Rinse shaped nozzles under the tap or they will become blocked with dried paint.

RECOMMENDED PAINTS

39 Gel paints, page 44

RECOMMENDED GLASS

All glass surfaces

37 Solvent-based pearl paints

Solvent-based pearl paints are designed to flow smoothly onto glass and are available in a variety of colours. They can be mixed together so you can achieve different shades of colours and even make your own colours.

PAINT TECHNIQUES

26 Using a fine brush, page 38

29 Using pipettes, page 39

Applying paint

Pearl paint is just dropped onto glass from a fine brush. Use the tip of the bristles to nudge the paint up to the outliner. Be liberal with the paint for the best results.

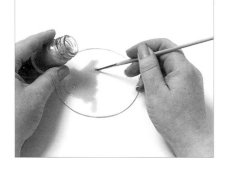

Combining colours

A single colour will have a metallic effect when dry. However, pearl paints are shown to their best when you mix colours together. When the paint has dried it will have a mottled texture to it, which is useful when painting animals, fish or birds as it naturally mimics the textures of fur, scales and feathers.

I Drop the first colour onto the glass, then drop on a second colour, allowing the two to flow together.

2 Add further colours as required.

I

2

Adding highlights

By adding white pearl to coloured pearl paint as it is drying you can create highlights, which make the paint come alive. Once you get the feel of the paint, you can control the effects. One way of doing this is to delay mixing the paints together. The longer you wait to drop white paint into a colour, the less it will spread. This effect can look quite astounding. The timing depends on how much paint you use and how warm the atmosphere is: the hotter it is the quicker the paint dries so the faster you have to work. But in general you have between I and I5 minutes to play with. You may also go back and drop some more paint in if it is spreading too quickly.

As the paint dries

'What are you doing?' asked a lady at an exhibition? 'Watching paint dry,' I replied. 'There's no need to be rude,' she reprimanded me. 'No, I really am watching paint dry,' I said.

I explained that I was watching pearl paint and that as it changes every few moments as it is drying, I never know what kind of fantastic finishes and textures I will end up with. All I can be sure of is that the effects will be stunning, as the paint has a life of its own. 'Oh look, it's changed while we have been talking,' she exclaimed, and we both settled down to watch it as if it was a favourite television programme.

△ White added immediately to wet purple paint.

△ White added after five minutes.

△ White added after ten minutes.

△ White added after fifteen minutes.

△ Wet pearl paint.

△ After drying for five minutes.

△ After drying for fifteen minutes.

△ After drying for one hour.

38 Solvent-based transparent paints

All solvent-based transparent paints have the same basic properties, but the base recipe will be different for each brand of paint, so be aware that you probably cannot mix different brands. They are seen as a more professional paint than the water-based paints, but they do have an odour so always use them in a room with good ventilation.

Applying paint

Drop the paint onto the glass with a fine brush. Use the tip of the bristles to nudge the paint up to the outlined edge of your design. You will nearly always need more paint than you think for the best results.

Let the paint dry naturally; do not try to dry it with a fan or hairdryer because this will just blow air bubbles into the paint.

Combining colours

To combine colours, drop the first colour onto the glass, then add the second colour, allowing the two to flow together.

Making opaque paint

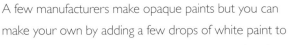

A few manufacturers make opaque paints but you can make your own by adding a few drops of white paint to coloured transparent paint. Mixing your own paint allows you to make it as dense or translucent as you want. The more dense the paint, the less you will see through it. Add a few drops of white paint to any transparent paint.

Give the bottle a good shake, but remember to let the bubbles disperse before you use it.

▽ *Half of this circle of glass has been painted with the opaque paint and half with ordinary transparent paint. You can see how opaque the paint is by how much less clearly you can see the design underneath that half.*

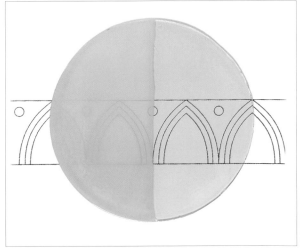

Adding highlights

Adding clear transparent paint to coloured transparent paint creates highlights that help to make your painting look less flat. You can change the effects of the highlights by adding paint at different times. The longer the main colour is left before the clear paint is added, the denser the highlight will be because the main colour will have thickened and dried a little, so the highlight won't spread so far.

△ *Clear added immediately to wet green paint.*

△ *Clear paint added after five minutes.*

△ *Clear paint added after ten minutes.*

△ *Clear paint added after fifteen minutes.*

PAINT TECHNIQUES

26 Using a fine brush, page 38

29 Using pipettes, page 39

39 Gel paints

These give a thick, hand-made glass effect and are available in a variety of colours and in transparent and opaque finishes. Some gel paints are water-based and some are air-drying polyester-based. The latter are very thick, but some become more liquid when stirred.

The time the paint takes to dry varies depending on how thickly you apply it, but it can take from one to two weeks to dry completely. When the paints dry they may shrink slightly and have a satin finish, but you can make them shinier with a coat of varnish, or you can create a frosted effect by painting them with matt varnish. Gel paints mix well with other materials, such as glass beads and glass painting granules and if stencilled through thick foam board the design will be raised, giving a slightly three-dimensional effect.

If you want to peel a gel paint off glass after it has dried, you must have first given the glass a coat of anti-adherent varnish. We usually just brush on a coat of petroleum jelly and this seems to do the trick. However, do check the different manufacturer's instructions before you start.

Applying paint

One of the best ways of applying this paint is with a palette knife.

1 Squeeze the paint out of the tube.

2 Spread it over the glass with the knife.

1

2

Thinning paint

You can thin some of the water-based gels down by adding water. Squeeze the paint onto the glass, then add water with a brush.

USING OUTLINER WITH GEL PAINT

If you want to use ordinary outliner with gel paints, we find that it is best to use it when the outliner is fresh. Sometimes when the paint dries it shrinks and can distort your design.

Piping paint

You can also pipe the paint directly from the tube or from an outlining bag.

40 Water-based paints

There are various makes of water-based paint on the market and though they are generally very similar, don't assume that just because they are water-based, they are all safe for children. Always check the safety standards on the sides of the labels for child safety information.

These paints may be a little too fluid for use on rounded glass and, when dry, they may wash off easily if exposed to water, so they are best used for decorative purposes. You can varnish over your finished work to protect it if you want to.

PAINT TECHNIQUES
26 Using a fine brush, page 38
29 Using pipettes, page 39

Applying paint

You can flow the paint onto the glass with a fine brush. However, even though these are very good paints, the finish is generally not as good as you would achieve with a solvent-based paint.

Thinning paint

The paints may also be watered down with a few drops of water to create thinner patches, which look like highlights.

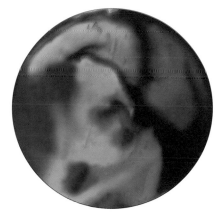

Combining colours

If you combine colours on the glass and then add water, they all run into each other, giving a beautiful stained-glass effect.

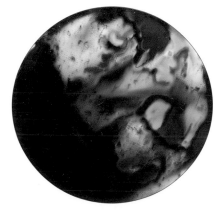

41 Pipe-and-peel paints

These are thick, creamy, water-based paints, which look a little like custard. Most of them are child-safe, but do check the label before letting children use them. Pipe-and peel paints are available in a range of colours and finishes.

PAINT TECHNIQUES

30 Using your fingers, page 39

33 Piping from the bottle, page 40

Applying paint

1 Apply the paint straight from the bottle. The paint will dry almost exactly as you put it on, so the more roughly you apply it, the more textured it will be.

2 To get a smooth finish, swirl the tip of a cocktail stick through the paint. This smooths it out and gets rid of air bubbles.

1

2

Combining colours

1 The colours mix well. Pipe different colours of paint onto the glass.

2 Pull the handle of a paintbrush through the different colours to create patterns.

1

2

Piping-and-peeling paint

1 Paint a shape onto a piece of glass (we painted a heart). When the paint is dry you can peel the shape off the glass.

2 The shape can then be stuck onto another glass item. This is very useful if you want to paint a curved item or a window. Just paint the shapes you want onto a conveniently flat piece of glass, then peel them off and stick them on the final item.

1

2

As the paint dries

The transparent pipe-and-peel paints are opaque when you squeeze them out of the bottle, but become transparent when dry. This piece of glass has been entirely painted with clear transparent paint, but half of it is dry, while the other half is still wet.

42 Oven-bake paints

Baking makes these paints much more durable and resistant to water. Some of them are even dishwasher-safe, but not all manufacturers recommend this. Oven-bake paints are available in various colours and finishes, including transparent, opaque, iridescent, and frosted-effect. The surface you paint them onto must be de-greased and clean before you start and able to be heated.

You must let the paints dry completely before baking an item. The time depends on the thickness of the paint, but it will be at least twenty-four hours. Otherwise, when baked, the moisture in the paint will make bubbles in the surface.

Bake the painted item in a domestic oven, following the manufacturer's instructions. Baking time is usually around thirty minutes from reaching the right temperature. But the glass must be placed in a cold oven so that it heats slowly and does not crack. Do not bake it at too high a temperature or for too long, as it may discolour. Let the glass cool down in the oven as a sudden temperature change may crack it. After baking, the paint will have a gloss finish.

Applying paint

Brush the paint onto the glass with a fine or thick brush.

▷ *You can also sponge or stipple oven-bake paints onto glass.*

Combining colours

If you apply one colour and you want to apply another, let the first coat dry for 10 to 15 minutes first. Sponging is a good way of achieving a graduated effect with these paints.

PAINT TECHNIQUES

26 Using a fine brush, page 38
27 Using a thick brush, page 38
28 Using a stippling brush, page 39
31 Using a sponge, page 40
32 Using plastic wrap, page 40

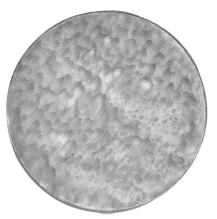

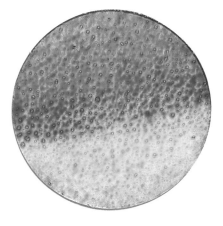

> **BAKING PAINTED ITEMS**
> When baking big pieces of glass, we usually give them ten minutes longer than recommended for the best result.

43 Air-drying polyester-based paints

These are a variety of permanent enamel paints for glass and tiles, though they do not work well on plastic and some treated glass. They are available in various colours and finishes including shimmer, satin, frost, glitter and frosted or etched-effect. None of these are very transparent, but there is also a smooth, transparent glass paint and a thick, textured gel glass paint.

The good thing about these paints is that when you have finished your project you can wash it, put it in the dishwasher and even put it in an oven up to 300°F, as well as microwaving it. But, as with all good things, you have to be patient, as it takes ten days to dry properly. The paints are non-toxic, but to be extra safe, don't use them on items that will come into contact with food: if you want to paint a plate, paint it on the back.

Before you paint the glass, you must give it a coating of the manufacturer's surface conditioner. This makes the paint adhere well to the glass once it has dried. If you have applied one colour of paint and you want to add another colour on top, you must let the first coat dry for 10 to 15 minutes first. If you are still painting your project after four hours, you must apply another coat of the surface conditioner, as it will have dried out.

Wash your brush out in water when you have finished painting, but don't get water into the paint, as it will cause it to granulate.

Applying paint

Brush on the paint, and the surface conditioner, with a soft, thick nylon brush. For this type of paint you should use synthetic bristle brushes.

Combining colours

You can combine different colours of paint straight onto the glass. However, this paint does not mix well with other types of paint.

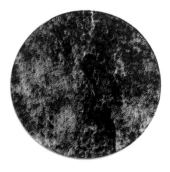

∧ *You get a good effect with these paints if you sponge them on.*

44 Light bulb paints

Some glass paints can be used on light bulbs, but you will have to check with the manufacturer first as to whether they are suitable. However, there are paints that are specially made for this purpose. These are best painted onto a low-wattage bulb, but can be used on a bulb up to 40 watts. Depending on the thickness of the paint, you must leave it a few days to dry completely. Do not be tempted to dry it by switching on the light bulb – the paint will tend to go brown and bubble. Even after a few days of drying, you may get a small brown spot at the top of the bulb, where it is very hot.

When you first switch the light bulb on, it may smoke a little and give off an odour. This is because the outliner and paint are not completely dry, but it will stop in time. Just leave it on for a short while until it stops smelling.

Applying paint

It is best to apply the paint with a soft brush or a sponge. The paint dries fast but it does smell, so do keep the room well ventilated. If you have enough paint you can dip the light bulbs into it and hang them up to dry.

Building up colour

Build up the density of colour you require by applying thin coats of paint, letting them dry in between. This circle of glass has been painted with different thickness of yellow paint.

Combining colours

To create a rainbow, simply brush on stripes of paint with a small brush, allowing the edges to blend together if you want a softer look, or letting each colour dry for a few minutes if you want more defined stripes.

PAINT TECHNIQUES

26 Using a fine brush, page 38

31 Using a sponge, page 40

32 Using plastic wrap, page 40

45 Brushing paints

What does this term mean? Well, we use it to refer to any of those paints that lend themselves to being brushed onto the glass easily. They can be in any of the paint mediums, but they are generally the thicker types of paint that do not flow very well. For example, most solvent-based paints flow easily, but there are thicker types that work better if you brush them on to the glass. These are best used for working on rounded surfaces, as when you paint them on they don't drip everywhere.

We know some painters who leave the lids off their paints for a few days so that they evaporate slowly until they get to the right brushing consistency. However, brushing paint on does leave brush marks, so these paints are no good if you want a smooth, flat surface.

Applying paint

Just brush the paint onto the glass with a thick brush.

Combining colours

Because brushing paints are thicker, when they are mixed with other colours they may become very dark and muddy looking. Therefore, brush them on with as little an overlap as possible.

 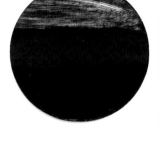

46 Luminous paints

Many manufacturers now have luminous paints in their range and some have luminous outliners. They are available in water-based, solvent-based and acrylic mediums and are used in the same way as other paints, but they do not come into their own until the light goes out.

You could incorporate luminous paints into a lamp design, so that when you switch the light off the luminous paint will glow. Or, you could make designs to stick on the window for Halloween.

Applying paint

Brush the paint onto the glass with a suitable brush for the paint medium.

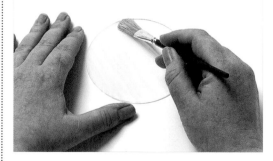

47 Frosting paints

If you prefer not to use etching cream, you can create similar effects with frosting paint. However, while the etching cream leaves a permanent finish, the frosting paint is only sitting on the surface and can be removed.

You can make your own frosting paint by mixing one part of clear water-based varnish with one part of white water-based paint.

PAINT TECHNIQUES

26 Using a fine brush, page 38

28 Using a stippling brush, page 39

29 Using pipettes, page 39

31 Using a sponge, page 40

32 Using plastic wrap, page 40

Painting

Flowing frosting paint can be brushed on with a fine brush. The finished effect is a fine, even frost.

Sponging

Thicker paints can be sponged or stippled on, or applied from the tube. The finished effect is more textured.

Spraying

Spray frosting paint is ideal for stencilling. Cut a plastic stencil and tape or spray-glue it in position. I

1 Spray over the stencil with the frosting paint, following the manufacturer's instructions.

2 Carefully peel off the stencil to reveal the frosted design.

1

2

48 Acrylic glass paints

We use this paint a lot on plastic films, as it stays malleable when dry and does not crack when you bend the film. It is, therefore, excellent for mobiles or film inserts in greetings cards. The colours mix together well, but if you paint a second colour over dry paint, the wet paint will dissolve the dry layer.

Applying paint

We usually brush it on quite thinly or it will look a bit cloudy when it dries.

△ *If you use this paint on film, when it is dry you can bend the film and the paint won't crack.*

PAINT TECHNIQUES

26 Using a fine brush, page 38

28 Using a stippling brush, page 39

31 Using a sponge, page 40

32 Using plastic wrap, page 40

PAINTING AND PAINTS **51**

49 Artist's acrylic paints

These paints can be used on glass and are excellent for imitating toleware or canal art. Acrylic paints are available in a huge range of colours and finishes and we use a lot of the metallic ones on pieces such as butterfly wings.

Applying paint

Brush the paint straight onto the glass for an opaque, solid colour.

Thinning paint

If you thin the paint by brushing water into it, you get a more transparent effect.

PAINT TECHNIQUES

26 Using a fine brush, page 38

27 Using a thick brush, page 38

28 Using a stippling brush, page 39

31 Using a sponge, page 40

32 Using plastic wrap, page 40

△ *Artist's acrylic paint brushed on in different thicknesses and with water added to some areas.*

△ *Purple metallic paint with water added to thin it down and give an iridescent effect.*

△ *A combination of assorted metallic paints. You can create some interesting textures and effects with these.*

50 Iridescent paints

These paints are available in most mediums. They are a creamy colour when wet, but when dry they take on other colours. If you gently streak these paints together, you get a multi-coloured, changing piece of glass. This effect is ideal for butterfly wings or the sheen on some bird's feathers.

51 Metallic paints

We use these to give painted glass a richer look or to add highlights to a project. You can also use them anywhere you would use metal leaf. The paints mix well together, so if you streak them you can get some interesting effects.

You should give the paints a good stir and shake before you use them, as they tend to have sediment at the bottom.

PAINT TECHNIQUES

26 Using a fine brush, page 38

27 Using a thick brush, page 38

28 Using a stippling brush, page 39

30 Using your fingers, page 39

31 Using a sponge, page 40

32 Using plastic wrap, page 40

Applying paint

Paint on solvent-based iridescent paints (these are the kind we usually use) with a fine brush.

PAINT TECHNIQUES

26 Using a fine brush, page 38

29 Using pipettes, page 39

△ *Held flat, the paint looks white.*

◁ *Tip the glass to one side and the light reflecting off the paint gives it a pink tint.*

▷ *Tip the glass to the other side and the tint changes to green.*

Metallic paint

Brush the paint onto the glass straight from the bottle.

△ *Gold paint.*

△ *Silver paint.*

APPLYING GILT CREAM TO OUTLINER
If you want to gild several pipe-and-peel outlined shapes, outline them on to a single sheet of glass and then rub the gilt cream over all of them with your finger.

Metallic cream

To apply gilt cream, squeeze a little out of the tube onto the glass and then spread it with your finger.

If you don't have any gold outliner, you can use gilt cream to turn black outliner gold. Dip a cotton bud into the cream and wipe it over the outliner.

PAINT TECHNIQUES

26 Using a fine brush, page 38

30 Using your fingers, page 39

△ *The big dolphin has been gilded while the smaller one remains black.*

52 Hobby enamel paints

You really don't have to stick to specially made glass paints. Almost every other paint on the market may be used in glass painting in one way or another – so do experiment.

Applying paint

Good ones to try are the hobby enamel paints. They look work well if you want to imitate canal art on glass. Brush on the paint with a fairly stiff-bristled brush.

PAINT TECHNIQUES

26 Using a fine brush, page 38

27 Using a thick brush, page 38

Combining colours

Hobby enamel paints don't really blend together very well, but, with a steady hand, you can butt colours up closely together.

Painting detail

These paints are excellent for painting detail or patterns on glass. Use a fine brush.

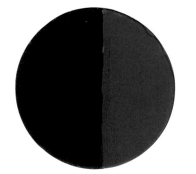

53 Household emulsion paints

We use white matt emulsion paint for painting snow onto glass. You can water the paint down a little and dip glass baubles into it to make perfect glass snowballs.

Applying paint

Emulsion paint is often available in sample pots, which are ideal as you rarely need a lot of paint, and they even have a built-in brush. For a flat, opaque finish, just brush the paint straight onto the glass.

PAINT TECHNIQUES

27 Using a thick brush, page 38

28 Using a stippling brush, page 39

31 Using a sponge, page 40

Combining colours

You can streak emulsion paints together as long as the edges of both colours are wet.

Sponging

You can achieve interesting effects by sponging, or stippling, emulsion paint onto glass.

54 Household gloss paints

Household gloss paints are good for stencilling onto glass and they can be diluted with thinners to create a more transparent effect.

Applying paint

For an opaque, shiny finish, brush the paint onto the glass with a soft-bristled brush.

PAINT TECHNIQUES

26 Using a fine brush, page 38

27 Using a thick brush, page 38

Combining colours

Like hobby enamels, gloss paints don't really blend together well, but you can butt colours up against one another.

Painting detail

Gloss paints are also good for painting detail or patterns on glass. Use a fine brush.

55 Combining different paints

Most manufacturers will say that you can only mix paints from the same range together, which generally is true, but you can get some interesting effects by experimenting with different paints. However, remember that when you mix different paints, you are altering their properties and you may affect them in the long-term as well as immediately – so don't blame the manufacturers afterwards.

Applying paint

Paint a piece of glass with paint from one manufacturer, then paint on a design with paint from a different range.

▷ *Where the second paint has dried, it has created a crackle effect.*

PAINT TECHNIQUES

26 Using a fine brush, page 38

working with glass, plastic and film

We have been disappointed in the past with the image that glass painting has sometimes had: take a jam jar that costs nothing and make it into something that looks like nothing. We are not suggesting that you paint expensive lead crystal glass, personally we think that that would be inappropriate. However, we do think that glass painters are doing themselves a disservice if they just use very cheap glass. The choice of glass items on the market is immense: there is very stylish glassware just crying out to be painted and some fun, pre-formed glass pieces, such as animals and fruit, which can be enhanced with glass paint.

You can also make your own shapes by following a few simple rules and techniques. Cutting glass is an acquired skill, but it isn't that difficult, so do have a go. You don't have to buy any large, expensive machinery, most of the basic tools are affordable. However, don't forget that glass can be sharp, so you must read the Safety with Glass section on page 57 before you start.

Coloured glass, textured glass, mirror glass and glass bevels can all be painted as well.

There are also plastic films on the market that are a real boon to the glass painter. Light-weight and sticky or flexible, they allow you to paint in ways that weren't previously possible.

Also discussed in this section are glues, to help you make flat glass shapes into three-dimensional objects, and varnishes for protecting your work.

56 Safety with glass

It is very important to take care when working with glass. I have been using it for years and no matter how careful you are, you can get the occasional cut. Always follow these simple rules for a safer working environment.

- Keep a First Aid box in your work area and replace anything you use from it.
- You can minimise the risk of a cut by wearing gloves when handling glass.
- If you are cutting or drilling glass with electrical equipment, make sure that it is plugged into a trip switch. This will protect you if the appliance develops a fault or if there is a sudden power surge.
- Glass drills normally use water to keep the drill bit cool; make sure that the plug is kept away from all sources of water.
- Electrical appliances should be fitted with a guard – make sure that it is in position.
- Wear safety glasses when cutting glass.
- Keep your work area tidy. Place off-cuts of glass in a bucket to prevent dangerous waste accumulating.

57 Working with glass

There are four main types of glass – plain glass, textured glass, coloured glass and mirror glass. Each of these is interesting to the glass painter, as they each have different qualities that can be used to good effect.

Plain Glass

Plain, clear glass comes in assorted thicknesses. The type of project you are working on will determine the thickness of glass you use. For suncatchers and glued shapes it is best to use 2mm- (1/16in-) thick glass, as it needs to be light in weight. For trinket boxes we use 3mm- (1/8in-) or 4mm- (3/16in-) thick glass. For large windows and more substantial pieces 6mm- (1/4in-) thick glass should be your choice, as it has a much greater overall strength.

> USING TOUGHENED GLASS
> For certain projects, such as tables, doors or windows, you will need to use toughened safety glass – this is a legal requirement but it is also good common sense.

Textured Glass

Glass comes with various textures and finishes. Abstract patterns, flowers and leaves or geometric designs can all be used in different projects.
If you want to paint directly onto patterned glass, paint on the flat side. If you paint on the textured side, all the texture in the glass will be filled in by the paint.

▷ *Leaf and flower patterned glass.*

▷ *The texture on this glass looks like bark.*

▷ *An abstract pattern on glass.*

Coloured Glass

You can paint onto coloured glass with pearl or opaque paints, though, of course, the design will only show on one side. The household opaque paints – emulsion, gloss, enamel and acrylic – can also be used. Opalescent glass can be lovely to paint on, but it is expensive to buy and sometimes has an uneven surface.

▷ *A favourite colour for glass – cobalt blue.*

▷ *Orange glass.*

▷ *Pale, opalescent glass.*

Mirror Glass

Mirror glass comes in various thicknesses and tints. Be aware that tinted mirror glass will influence the colours of the paints you use. You can paint directly onto mirror glass, but you will have to use carbon paper to transfer the design (see 7 Transferring designs onto mirror glass, page 24).
You can strip the backing off mirror with specialist products.

▷ *Bevelled edge mirror.*

▷ *Smoky grey mirror.*

▷ *Amber mirror.*

58 Cutting straight lines in glass

You need an adjustable T-square, preferably a metal one, and a hand-held glass cutter to cut straight lines. You can use a ruler instead of a T-square, but they do have a tendency to slip, which will spoil your cut. It is worth buying the best tools you can afford as, in this instance, good tools will make the task easier.

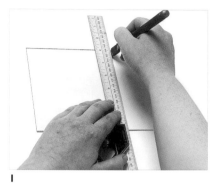

1

2

3

4

5

1 Lay the T-square on the glass where you want to cut. Make sure the cross-piece is butted up to the edge of the glass so that it won't slip. Position the glass cutter against the far edge of the glass, tight up against the T-square.

2 Push the cutter down onto the glass to notch the edge, then applying firm pressure, score one continuous line across the glass. Only do this once, don't be tempted to go over it again or it will not break smoothly.

3 Place the piece of glass on top of a ruler, with the scored line against one edge. Holding one side of the glass securely, apply gentle pressure to the other side until it snaps. If the glass is quite thick, you may find it easier to lay it over the edge of a table and snap it with pliers. Wearing glass gloves will minimise the risk of a cut.

4 Using a sanding pad, smooth off all the sharp edges. Simply run the pad a few times over each edge, on both sides of the glass.

5 Don't forget to smooth all the corners, as they will be especially sharp.

HOLDING THE GLASS CUTTER
Hold the glass cutter like a pen, but keep it upright when scoring glass so that the cutting wheel stays in contact with the surface of the glass. Keep the cutter well-oiled so that it always runs smoothly.

BUYING AN ELECTRIC GLASS SANDER
If you do a lot of glass cutting, it may be advisable to treat yourself to an electric glass sander. This will sand the edges of glass to either an etched finish or it will polish them smooth.

59 Cutting glass bottles

Those of you with a recycling inclination should try using a bottle cutter. Overcome the urge to throw it through a window because your first bottles snap in the wrong places and persevere – it can be done. You can turn beautifully shaped wine bottles into impromptu vases and vessels. Don't forget to throw your rejects in the bottle bank though.

60 Cutting glass circles

It is difficult to cut out a perfect circle by hand, so invest in a circle cutter. You can even buy some that do ovals as well.

1 Set the circle cutter to the size of circle you require. Stick the central suction pad to the surface of the glass, then, with one continuous movement, sweep the cutting wheel around in a circle on the glass. Do this just once, then remove the cutter.

2 With a hand-held glass cutter, score three or four evenly spaced lines around the circle, running from just outside the scored circle line to the edge of the glass.

3 Pick up the piece of glass and, using the handle of the glass cutter, gently tap around the scored circle line, on the back of the glass. You will see the score lines crack as you tap.

4 The waste glass may just fall away, but if it doesn't, apply gentle pressure with your hands. Sand the sharp edge of the circle smooth.

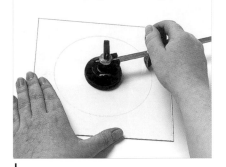

1

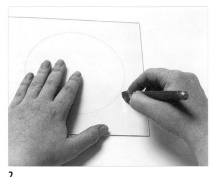

2

3

4

LEAVING WASTE GLASS AROUND DESIGNS
When cutting circles or shapes from glass, always allow waste glass around the design. This makes it easier to snap the score lines. If the area of waste glass is too small, the scored line will tend to snap badly and chip easily.

1 Set the bottle cutter to the height you want then, with the cutting wheel pressed hard against the glass, revolve the bottle slowly to score a continuous line.

2 Place the bottle in a bowl or sink and carefully pour very hot water into it, to just above the scored line.

3 You will hear a crack and the top will just lift off the bottle. Pour away the water and sand the sharp edges of the glass.

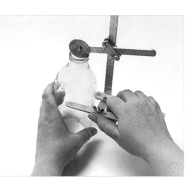

1

2

3

BREAKING THE BOTTLE
If the bottle does not crack, pour out the water and refill it with more hot water. You may also help it along by giving the scored line a gentle tap with the handle of a hand-held glass cutter.

61 Cutting glass shapes

Once you have mastered straight and circle cuts, have a go at some freehand cutting. Try to simplify your designs so that you can cut them out in one go, though you can do two or three cuts if necessary.

STANDING IN THE RIGHT SPOT
Before you start cutting, work out where to stand so that you can score right round the template with one continuous movement.

1 Place a template of the shape you want to cut out under the glass. Using a hand-held glass cutter and starting at the bottom of the design, score the glass all the way around the template with one continuous line.

2 Score a few evenly spaced lines from just outside the scored template line to the edge of the glass.

3 Pick up the piece of glass and, using the handle of the glass cutter, gently tap around the scored template line, on the back of the glass. You will see the score lines crack as you tap.

4 The waste glass may just fall away, but if it doesn't, apply gentle pressure with your hands. Sand the sharp edges of the shape smooth.

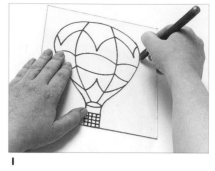

1

2

3

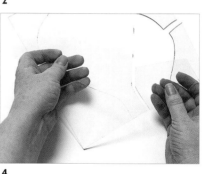

4

62 Drilling holes in glass

Professional glass drills have water feeds to keep the drill bit cool. However, we use an ordinary pillar drill, a glass drill bit and a rubber washer to hold a reservoir of water and this works well for us. Do be careful when using water and electricity together: plug your drill into a safety trip switch, even if you are only using a few drops of water.

1 Mark the glass where you want the hole to be and place a rubber washer over the mark. Then, pour a little water into the hole of the washer. This is important as the water helps to keep the drill bit cool.

2 Drill just halfway through the glass – do not apply too much pressure, let the drill do the work. Lift the drill bit out of the glass and remove the washer.

3 Turn the glass over and carefully line up the half-drilled hole with the drill bit. Replace the washer and refill it with water, then drill into the glass again until you cut right through.

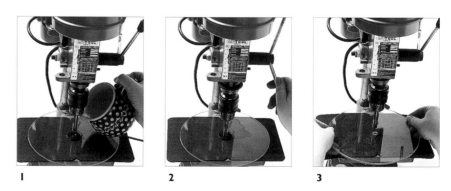

1

2

3

USING A DRILL ON GLASS
Set the drill to the speed the manufacturer recommends and keep the drill bits sharp with a special stone sharpener for the best results.

63 Working with plastic

There are a variety of thicknesses and textures of plastic that can be used in place of glass. Some paints may react with plastic, so experiment on a scrap piece before starting a project. We use rigid plastic a lot in our three-dimensional projects because if you have a large picture with four or five sheets of glass in it, it can be too heavy to hang on the wall. We also use plastic a lot for making mobiles and creating textured sheets of thick, water-based paint.

DEALING WITH STATIC ELECTRICITY
If you want to outline onto the plastic, remove the protective covering well in advance, or the static electricity generated by peeling off the covering will make your outliner dance a jig. Wiping the plastic with an anti-static cloth will help to reduce the static.

1 To cut a straight line across a piece of thin plastic, use a metal ruler and a cutting mat and score the plastic heavily with a heavy-duty craft knife – be careful of your fingers.

2 Use both hands to snap the plastic along the scored line.

3 If the plastic has a protective covering, leave it on until you have cut the piece you want, then just peel it off.

If you want to cut a shape or thicker plastic, you will need to use a jigsaw. Sand the cut edges carefully with fine sandpaper, making sure not to mark the surface of the plastic.

1

2

DRILLING INTO PLASTIC
Drilling holes into plastic is almost as easy as drilling into wood. However, we find a piece of masking tape stuck onto the plastic where you are drilling stops the drill bit from sliding.

3

△ Textured plastic can provide an interesting background for glass painting.

64 Using varnishes

Solvent-based paints are very tough and will resist most sources of damage. These don't really need to be varnished, but you may want to varnish water-based paints to help protect them.

A few paint manufacturers produce their own varnishes. We find that water-based acrylic or water-based polyurethane varnishes are good, but choose one that states that it will not go yellow. We have also used yacht varnish, though always make sure that the varnish you choose will not react to the paint. Apply the varnish with a soft brush so as not to leave brush strokes and we usually apply two or three coats.

65 Using ultra-violet glue

When this glue is dry it is completely invisible. This makes it perfect for gluing glass bevels to mirror glass or plain glass, as shown here. Ultra-violet glue is also good for gluing two pieces of glass together to form a stand, for a clock or a picture frame.

1 Work away from direct sunlight or the glue will start to harden before you are ready. Squeeze glue onto the glass where you want to stick the bevel.

2 Place the bevel on the glued glass or mirror. Gently move it a tiny amount, pressing down to squeeze out any air bubbles.

3 Place an ultraviolet light over the top of the glass, switch it on and leave it for 20 or 30 seconds, until the glue has gone hard. Wear special safety glasses and make sure that you don't look at the ultra-violet light. If you don't have an ultra-violet lamp, place the glass in direct sunlight on a windowsill for a few minutes.

4 Cut away any excess glue from around the bevel with a craft knife. Glass bevels are excellent for embellishing mirrors and are available either in design packs or loose (see Suppliers, page 190). We sometimes drill a small hole into the top of a bevel, then paint, etch or even sandblast it and use it as a suncatcher.

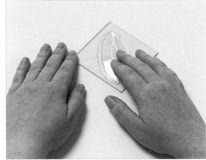

1

2

3

4

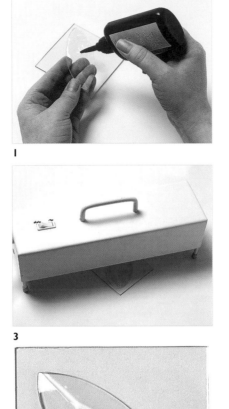

△ Bevel glued to plain glass.

△ Bevel glued to mirror glass.

66 Using epoxy glue

Two-part, fast-drying, clear epoxy glue can be used for gluing picture frames or clock stands, and is ideal for attaching glass nuggets or marbles. However, when dry it is not as invisible as ultra-violet glue.

Brands of epoxy glue vary, so read the instructions before you start. Mix up the glue on a piece of paper or card, using a cocktail stick. Use the stick to dab the glue onto the glass, then hold the glued pieces together for a few minutes while the glue dries.

67 Using silicone glue

We like using this glue because it is thick and tacky and gives you time to position the glass. Also, if you make a mistake it is easy to cut the pieces of glass apart again with a craft knife. Silicone glue comes in a variety of colours, but we usually use clear glue. This is milky when it comes out of the tube, but it does turn clear when dry.

This glue comes in small or very large containers, which are cheaper to buy but impossible to handle. So, we turn to our reliable outlining bags and just fill one of those up from a large container. Shown here is the technique used for making a simple glass box using silicone glue.

1 Firstly, you need five identical squares of glass. Pipe silicone glue onto one edge of a square of glass and rest it on something, we used a roll of masking tape. Then, pipe glue onto two edges of a second square of glass.

2 Lay a third square of glass (which will be the bottom of the box) flat on the worksurface. Place the first piece of glass, glued edge down, edge-to-edge onto the bottom square and at right angles to it.

3 Place the second square onto the bottom square, with one glued edge against the bottom and one against the first square. Hold the squares together for a few minutes until the glue starts to cure, then leave it to dry for ten minutes. Add the remaining two sides of the box in the same way, ensuring that each join is glued.

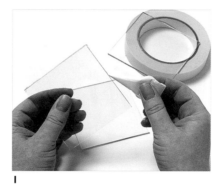

1

2

3

CLEANING UP JOINS
Use a craft knife to easily remove any bits of silicone glue that have oozed out of the joins and dried on the glass.

WHAT TO USE SILICONE GLUE FOR
This glue is ideal for making the separators for sheets of glass in three-dimensional work and making trinket boxes. It is also especially good for sticking wings to butterflies and fairies, because the silicone stays flexible and so the wings move if they get a waft of air.

Don't use silicone glue for making picture frame stands – it doesn't dry quickly enough and so the picture frame tends to move on the stand.

68 Thick film

A thicker plastic film is now available that can be used in place of glass for some projects. As the film is flexible, it is very versatile: for instance you can use it to make mobiles or jewellery. We have chosen to demonstrate this film by making a three-dimensional, hanging butterfly. You outline and paint onto the flat film, then make the most of its flexibility and bend the butterfly into shape

1

2

3

4

5

1 Place the thick film over the template and outline in the usual way (see 2 How to outline, page 19).

2 Fill the butterfly's body in with extra outliner, then push one end of a length of wire into this outliner. The free end of the wire must be towards the head. Leave to dry so that the wire is firmly embedded in the body.

3 Paint the butterfly, section by section, in the usual way (see Painting and paints, pages 36-55).

4 When the paint is dry, cut the butterfly out with sharp scissors.

5 Then bend the film to fold the wings upwards. Tie some thread to the wire and hang the butterfly up. You can bend the wire further to balance the butterfly properly once it is flying.

69 Self-adhesive film

One of the most exciting films is a self-adhesive film that is now available. When the clear backing is peeled off and the design is stuck on the glass, it will stay there as long as you want it to. You can peel it off again, but it will lose some of its adhesive properties.

70 Cling film

Another useful film is this one that can be repositioned easily, so you can peel a design on and off a window or other glass item, many times. This film is especially good for children's designs, or for temporary or seasonal designs that can be peeled off, stored and reused.

1 Place a design under the film and outline it in the usual way (see 2 How to outline, page 19).

2 Paint the design (see Painting and paints, pages 36-55). When the paint was dry we over-outlined the design with gold outliner (see 4 Over-outlining, page 20).

3 When the design is completely dry, cut it out with sharp scissors.

4 Peel off the clear backing sheet.

5 Then position the design on your chosen glass item and press it down. If the position is not quite right, peel off and re-stick it, but remember, the more you handle it, the less sticky it will be.

1

2

3

4

WORKING ON THE RIGHT SIDE OF THE FILM

Before you start, make sure you are working on the film rather than the backing by peeling back a corner to reveal the sticky side. If you find this difficult, place a piece of sticky tape on either side of the film in one corner and use these to pull the film and backing apart.

5

1 Place the design onto a light box or piece of glass with a light under it so you can see through the backing card to outline it. Outline in the usual way (see 2 How to outline, page 19). You can peel the film off the backing card to outline the design, but we find that the film tends to wrinkle if you do. Don't make the design too big or its own weight will pull it off the glass.

2 Paint the design (see Painting and paints, pages 36-55).

3 When the paint is dry, cut the design out and peel off the backing card.

4 Lay the design onto any flat, vertical or curved glass surface and it will cling to it. The design can be removed and repositioned as often as you like.

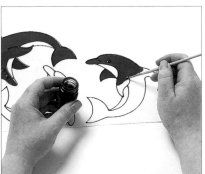
1

2

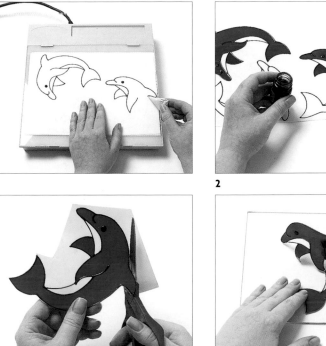
3

4

etching

For years, we were always a bit afraid to use etching media, thinking it was like battery acid. It is nothing like it at all, but it is a mild corrosive. It needs to be respected, so always follow all the safety instructions on the container.

Always wear rubber gloves and goggles, in case you splash some cream. If you get some on your skin, wash it off straightaway with plenty of cold running water. When I first got cream on my skin, I just wiped it off and didn't wash it. An hour or so later I had a rash and blister. So now if I get it on my skin, I wash it off and all is well. With this in mind, never let children use etching media and don't use it when they are in the room.

Etching media comes as a cream, which you just brush onto the glass, or as a paste, which is best applied with a spatula, or even a silk screen. We always use the cream, which takes from between one and five minutes to etch glass, depending on the brand you use. When the recommended time has elapsed, wash the cream off with cold water and you will see your design etched onto the glass.

Etching creams can be pink, purple, blue or white in colour, but they are all basically the same. You can brush them on, dip into them or stipple and stencil with them. Etching cream does not work well on plastic, acrylic, acetate or film, or any glass that has a finish on it, such as lustre glass.

We have placed coloured glass under the etched designs in this section so you can see them clearly.

71 Peel-off outliner as an etching mask

Choose a pipe-and-peel outliner to mask the glass with, as it will be easy to lift off again once you have completed the etching process.

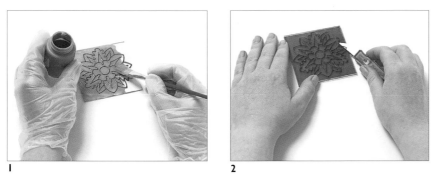

1 Outline your design onto glass (see How to outline, page 19) and let it dry. Then, with a thick brush, paint the cream all over the glass and outliner and leave it for recommended time before washing it off.

2 Peel off the outliner to reveal your clear glass design underneath. You may find a craft knife helpful for lifting up the corners. If you are very clever and peel off the outliner in one piece, you can stick it to another piece of glass and repeat the process.

---

72 Watered-down outliner as an etching mask

Squeeze outliner into a bottle and mix in some water, a few drops at a time until you get a nice brushing thickness. Then leave it for a while to let the bubbles disperse.

1 Outline the design (see 2 How to outline, page 19) and let it dry. Then, using watered-down outliner, fill in the areas of the design you want to remain clear. Leave it to dry

2 Brush the etching cream on over the glass and outliner. Leave it for the recommended time, then wash it off.

3 Peel off the outliner to reveal the design.

73 A pre-cut vinyl motif as an etching mask

These offer the easiest way to make a mask for etching, as long as you can find a design that you like.

1 Stick the vinyl motif onto the glass, pressing it down well. Brush the etching cream on over the glass and vinyl. Leave it for the recommended time, then wash the cream off.
2 Peel off the motif to reveal the etched design. You may need a craft knife to help you lift the corners of the vinyl motif.

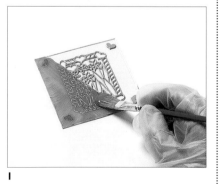

1

2

74 Lace effects with etching cream

This technique is simple, works well and looks fantastic, but you will need to practice a little first with a scrap of lace and a piece of old glass. Choose a cheap lace to work with as the cream may damage it. The lace has to absorb the cream, so choose a cotton rather than a nylon lace. The lace should be quite textured, but flat; a raised texture will mean that it won't touch the glass evenly.

75 Masking, stippling, sponging and stamping with etching cream

We have used all of these techniques on one sample, just to show you how to use them. You can, of course, use each one separately.

1 Place some paper underneath the lace and brush the etching cream all over it. Be quite generous, the cream must penetrate the lace.

2 Peel the lace off the dirty paper and lay it on a clean piece.

3 Lay the piece of glass you want to etch on top of the lace.

4 With one hand on the glass and the other under the paper, turn the whole thing over. Be careful that nothing slips

5 Now lay another piece of paper on top and then a book with something heavy on top of it (we used a jug of water). Leave it for the recommended time.

6 Remove the weight and the paper, peel back the lace and wash the cream off the glass.

1

2

3

4

3

4

5

6

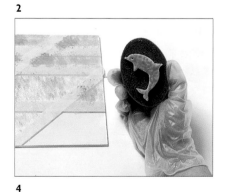

1

2

3

1 Stick the masking tape onto the glass in any design you wish.

2 Apply the etching cream to some of the un-masked areas with a stippling brush. It doesn't matter if the cream goes onto the tape.

3 Sponge cream onto other areas.

4 Dab etching cream onto a pre-cut sponge.

5 Press the sponge gently onto a clear area of glass. Leave the cream for the recommended time, then wash it off and peel off the tape.

4

5

special paint effects

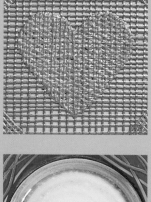

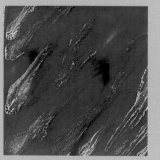

Glass paints are amazingly versatile, as you can see from the special effects shown in this section. Tilt them, layer them, float them, marble them – if you have an idea, try it – the effects may be fantastic. Don't feel tied down to using one type of paint: mix them together, it may not always work, but on the other hand, it might look wonderful.

Tilt painting is very easy to do; as soon as you have mastered flowing paint onto glass, you are ready to try it. The other techniques in this section, however, do require a little practice. This is particularly true of Layering: you really must have perfected your outlining skills before you try this technique. If your lines are wobbly or broken, the layered effect just won't work properly.

Marbling with water can be messy, so do lay down newspaper to protect your worksurface and wear old clothes. It can take a few goes to get a good effect with this technique, but persevere as when it does work, it looks great.

This section of the book, and the next one, *Stamped, printed and textured effects*, are both designed to not only introduce you to some of the effects you can get by using glass paints creatively, but also to inspire you to come up with your own ideas. We are great believers in experimentation; it is how we developed many of the unique techniques included in this book. So please do break all the rules, including any we may have set down in these pages, and see what happens.

76 Tilt painting

If you are using flowing glass paints, you will have to spend some time making sure that your work surface is totally flat, so as the paint dries it is nice and even. But if you want to create a shaded effect, use the tilt painting technique.

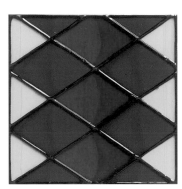

△ We did two tilts and painted the remaining areas with flat colour, but you can paint and tilt as often as you want on one design.

I Outline a design in the usual way (see 2 How to outline, page 19) and let it dry. With the glass flat, paint the first colour onto it.

2 Then place something underneath the glass on one side to tilt it a little: we used a ruler but you could use a coin or a thin piece of wood. You only need to lift the side of the glass a tiny amount – lift it too much and the paint will flow right over the outliner and onto the table. Once it is tilted you will see the paint flow to one side and start to thicken there. Leave it to dry like this.

3 Now repeat the process using another colour and tilting the glass in another direction. Leave it to dry.

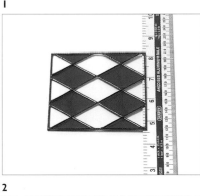

I

2

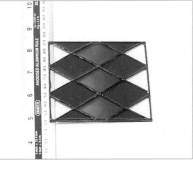

3

77 Layering

Warning – do not attempt this technique until you are confident of your outlining skills. As long as you can outline neatly, layering is essentially simple to do, but you must work carefully and let each layer dry before starting the next one, so it does take time. You can use any medium that will keep its shape when it is dry; outliner, textured paint or thick water-based paint will all work well.

I Fill an outlining bag with paint and pipe lines right across the glass in one direction. The lines should be parallel and as even as you can make them.

2 When the lines are dry, pipe another layer at right angles to the first layer. Fill another bag with a different coloured paint and continue to build up the layers in the same way. Always pipe the next layer of lines at an angle to all the previous layers.

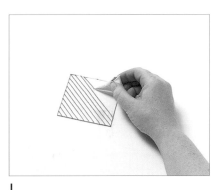

I

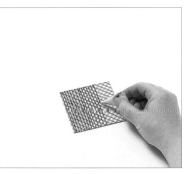

2

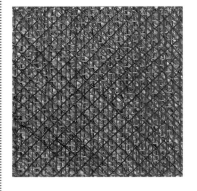

△ This finished sample has six layers of different-coloured paints in it: the result almost looks knitted.

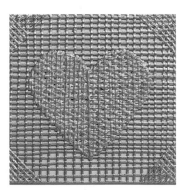

△ We used gold and silver outliner for this sample. The heart shape was piped on after the second layer and then filled in with more layers of straight lines.

78 Marbling with a brush

Because the white paint is very thick it shows up clearly when streaked into wet paint. As it dries it will spread a little and give a marbled effect.

Paint a piece of glass: we used royal blue and purple transparent paints. Then, while the paint is still wet, streak some white paint into it with a fine brush. You may have to experiment a little to determine the right amount of white paint to apply, but once you have got this right you can use this technique to create very sumptuous effects.

79 Using a turntable

You can use a turntable to good effect when you paint glass, especially if you want a smooth painted surface on a plate or bowl. You can use a turntable, a potter's wheel if you have one, or even an old record player, but be careful with the paint if you do.

1

2

1 Position your glass dead centre on the turntable. We don't know any tricks for doing this perfectly – just spin it around and use your eye. Now give it a good spin, making sure it revolves freely.

Choose a brushing paint – not a flowing one – and dip your brush into it. Start on the outside of the item and work inwards. Spin the turntable with one hand and just gently lay the paint-loaded brush onto the glass with the other. As it spins the paint will be distributed evenly. Repeat the process until you have enough paint

on the item. Then add another ring of colour: you can add as many rings as will fit within the first one.

2 Before the paint dries you can put a pattern into it by spinning the plate and dragging a cotton bud through the wet paint.

PAINTING PLATES
We painted onto the top of a glass plate but if you intend to use it for food, paint onto the back and give it a few coats of varnish to seal it.

80 Marbling with water

For this technique you must use a solvent-based paint that will float on the top of water. Use a bowl large enough to hold the item you want to marble. You want to get the item you are marbling covered with paint in the first dip to achieve a clean, marbled pattern.

1

2

LINING THE BOWL

Line the bowl you are using with a large plastic bag before you fill it with water. Then when you have finished, all you have to do is lift the bag out, make a small hole in the bottom to release the water and all the left-over paint will stick to the inside of the bag, which makes cleaning up so much easier.

DIPPING SEVERAL ITEMS

If you are dipping several items, just lay a few sheets of kitchen paper on top of the water between dips and the old paint will stick to these. Remove the paper and throw it away.

3

1 Fill the plastic-lined bowl with cold water.

2 Using a pipette, drip a few drops of each different-coloured paint you are using onto the water. You can use as many colours as you want, but we find that more than three colours can make the finished item look a bit muddy. You must work fairly fast, as you don't want the paint to dry on top of the water.

3 Take a cocktail stick and give the paint a swirl – not too much though.

4 You may want to wear rubber gloves for the actual dipping as it can be a bit messy. Position your glass item over the paint, ready to dip.

5 Then dip the glass into the water and take it out again in one smooth rolling motion – don't allow the water to come over the top of a plate or bowl. Leave the item to dry.

DOUBLE-DIPPING ITEMS

If you want to double-dip the item, let the first layer of paint dry before you attempt a second dip.

4

5

stamped, printed and textured effects

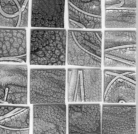

Of all the chapters in this book, this is the most inventive one. There is an enormous variety of paints available on the market today and the ways in which you can use them to create stamped, printed or textured effects are almost endless. Stencil or sponge with them, print or mark them – you can create a wide range of effects with paint. You can embed plastic and glass beads, slivers of other paints, or even lace or pulses, into a painted surface to give it an entirely new dimension.

Some of the techniques shown in this section, using metal leaf for example, might seem to be moving away from glass painting as such. However, metal leaf looks wonderful combined with both coloured outliner and glass paints and it will enhance many of your projects.

Why should glass paints always be used in two dimensions? We have included a three-dimensional technique in this section, showing you how to make flowers and leaves from glass paint. However, you can use the same method to make other shapes: maybe miniature Christmas trees as a table centrepiece, complete with piped baubles.

We have only given a selection of different techniques to inspire you, but the possibilities are as wide-ranging as your imagination, so don't just pick up a brush and paint: think of other ways you can use paints. If you have skills in any other arts or crafts, see if you can apply them to your glass painting – be brave and experiment.

81 Stencilling with brushing paint or outliner

Stencilling is a favourite craft for many people and it has a place in glass painting as well.

1 Lay the template under the stencil film and cut it out with a hot stencil cutter.

2 Spray the back of the stencil with low-tack adhesive and place it onto the glass.

3 Using a stippling brush, dab brushing paint or outliner over the stencil.

4 Peel off the stencil and leave the paint or outliner to dry.

1

2

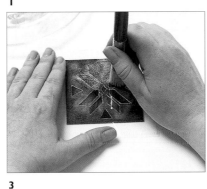

3

4

82 Stencilling with gel paint

To create a raised stencilled design, use thick stencil foam and gel paint. You can use one, or several, colours of paint in your design.

1 Draw or trace out the design onto stencil foam and cut it out with a craft knife on a cutting mat. Spray the back of the stencil with low-tack adhesive and lay it onto the glass. Squeeze gel paint out of the tube onto the stencil and spread it out with a palette knife. Leave to dry for about ten minutes.

2 Carefully peel off the template and leave the paint to dry completely. When it is dry, trim away any excess paint with a craft knife.

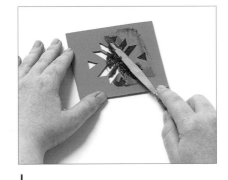

1

2

83 Making a stamp

You can make a stamp to any design, though remember that the image will come out back-to-front. So, if you want to stamp letters, you must make them backwards in order for them to come out forwards. You need to buy a stamping pad with ink that will adhere well to glass and not smudge. Ask your retailer for the right kind.

1 Outline your design onto thick film in the usual way (see 2 How to outline, page 19). Your outlining must be as smooth and even as possible to give you a clear stamp. When the outliner is dry, cut round it as closely as possible with sharp scissors.

2 Then cut out a piece of wood the same size as the design and apply some glue to one side of it. We usually use a glue gun for this, but you could use epoxy glue.

3 Stick the film to the wood.

4 Use your stamp as you would an ordinary rubber stamp (see 17 Stamping an outline, page 28). Press it onto the inkpad, then firmly onto the glass.

1

2

3

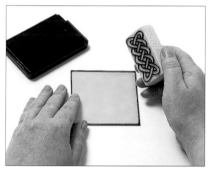

4

84 Printing

There are numerous objects you can use to print onto painted glass with: lace, flowers, wire, and in this case a leaf. Just pluck a leaf off a tree and wipe it clean.

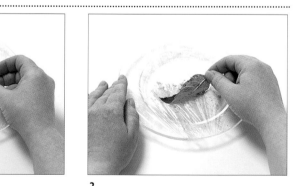

1

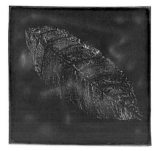

1 Thinly spread some outliner, gold in this case, onto a plastic-covered plate, then press the leaf onto the outliner.

2 Peel the leaf off the outliner and check that it is evenly coated.

3 Lay it onto the glass and press it down gently. Then just peel it off and you will be left with a gold leaf imprint.

3

85 Creating a stamped effect

When paint is nearly dry, depending on the paint you use, you can mark it with different implements, giving it a stamped look. You can use almost anything –

pens, forks, rubber stamps, modelling tools, wire mesh, cocktail sticks and much more – so do experiment.

The paint needs to have a dry, thick layer on the top and be softer underneath. Drag your chosen tool, in this case we used a fork, across a half dry piece of painted glass.

To get this right you have to know your paint, so do initial experiments and time them carefully

An alternative idea is to cover a piece of glass with textured paint, then immediately make your handprint on it. Make a family window with the whole family's hands or take imprints of a baby's hand as it grows up.

◁ This texture was created with a plastic scouring-pad

▷ Biscuit cutters were used to stamp this piece of glass.

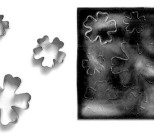

86 Embedding paint into paint

We were inspired to develop this paint effect after a trip to Milan where we saw the most beautiful glass windows and doors. They seemed to be made from slivers of different coloured glass between two pieces of plain glass. This is our miniature version of the effect.

1 Paint sheets of film with textured or flowing paints. Leave them to dry them cut them up into thin slivers. Alternatively, spread textured or gel paints over sheets of glass, let them dry and then peel them off. Cut the sheets into thin slivers.

1

2 Coat a piece of glass with a layer of clear paint.

3 Sprinkle the coloured strips onto the paint to make a design and let them dry into the paint. Paint the whole piece with one or more coats of clear paint.

2

3

USING GEL PAINT

You can use clear gel paint to embed the slivers in. This will give a textured look to the glass.

STAMPED, PRINTED AND TEXTURED EFFECTS   **77**

87 Embedding objects in paint

Try embedding things into glass paint – you can choose almost anything. You could paint a thin layer of clear paint and lay a coin in it. Leave it to dry and then paint over it with more clear paint. Choose a coin with the right date and it makes an interesting memento of a wedding or the birth of a baby.

1

2

I Outline a design (see 2 How to outline, page 19) and leave it to dry. Paint the first section of glass and, while the paint is still wet, drop a glass nugget into it then let it dry.

2 Paint the next section and drop a few more glass nuggets into it. As the paint dries it will hold the nuggets in position.

△ This is the same design, but with plastic granules dropped into the paint. When using these it is best to paint a section of each colour at a time and leave it to dry before you move onto the next section. It is also a good idea to drip some paint on top of the granules to really secure them.

△ This piece of glass was embedded with rice in the centre, yellow split peas for the petals and green lentils for the background. This would look good on a kitchen cupboard door or a storage jar where the pulses stuck to the outside showed you what was inside.

△ We embedded a piece of lace onto this square of glass. Take a large piece of lace and lay it over glass that has been coated with one layer of clear paint. Then, either tape it down to the worksurface so it does not move or tape it around the back of the glass, stretching it tight. Leave it to dry. Build up more thin layers of clear paint, one layer at a time, letting the paint dry between layers. If you put too much paint on at a time it will lift the lace off the glass and go wrinkly. When it is dry, remove the tape and trim away the edges of the lace with scissors.

△ This was made in the same way as the flower above, but with glass beads dropped onto the paint instead.

△ We made letters (see 91 Using moulds, page 81), then put them on the glass and painted over them with solvent-based paint to embed them.

88 Making mosaic

Glass mosaic tiles are expensive to buy, so make your own mosaic-effect tiles. Children will love making these, as they are so simple to do and they really do look great.

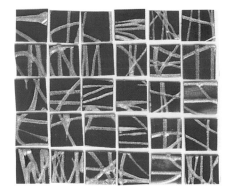

1 Paint sheets of self-adhesive clear film using any type of paint. Brush water-based paint all over the film to get the colour and texture you want. Or, squirt different colours of gel paint all over the film, then squidge it around with your finger: the more textured and rough the surface, the better the mosaic tiles will look when you cut them up. You can paint all over the film with mixed pearl paints. If you are using plain transparent or acrylic paint, try squirting lines of gold and silver outliner, or even textured paint, over the top. Below are the painted films we used.

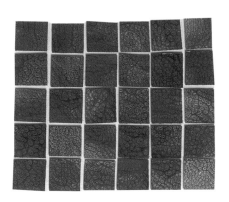

▷ *Red and orange pearl paints.*

▷ *Blue and green gel paints.*

▷ *Red solvent-based transparent paint and gold outliner.*

▷ *Blue and yellow pearl paints and gold outliner.*

2 When the film is dry, cut it into strips. Use a craft knife and metal ruler, but remember to use a cutting mat underneath so as not to damage your table.

3 Cut the strips into evenly sized squares. When you have a pile of different squares, arrange them on the glass and when you are happy with the pattern, peel off the backing and stick the squares down.

4 A speedier way of cutting squares is to cut strips, then peel the backing off and snip off squares with scissors. You have to stick the squares down immediately so only use this method if you are making a one-colour mosaic, or if you are very sure of your design.

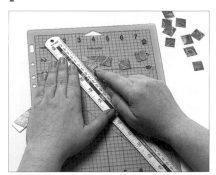

2

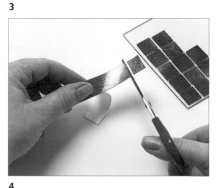

3

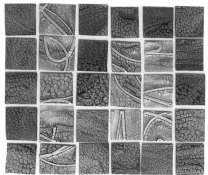

4

89 Using biscuit cutters

Using biscuit cutters, of which there are a vast assortment on the market, you can make flowers, leaves, gingerbread men – whatever you want. Use water-based pipe-and-peel paint and you can stick your cut-outs onto any glass surface. This is a simple way to make seasonal or party window decorations.

1 To make a gingerbread man, lay an appropriate biscuit cutter on a piece of paper and draw round it with a felt-tipped pen.

2 Place a sheet of glass on top of this drawn template and outline brown paint, straight from the bottle, onto the glass. Outline right around, and just outside, your pen line.

3 Fill in the gingerbread man with more of the same paint.

4 Smooth out the paint and take out any bubbles with a cocktail stick (see 40 Pipe-and-peel paints, page 46). Leave it to dry.

5 Position the biscuit cutter so that it sits within the painted shape.

6 Run a rolling pin (not too surprisingly, our rolling pin is made from glass) over the cutter to press it down through the paint. Lift the cutter off and peel away the excess paint. If there are any areas where the cutter has not gone right through the paint, then go over the line with a craft knife.

7 Pipe white features and buttons onto the gingerbread man and leave him to dry. Last of all, add the pupils to his eyes.

1

2

3

4

5

6

7

90 Using aluminium foil

We use aluminium foil in various ways. At the back of three-dimensional pictures it helps to reflect light back into the picture. Small balls of foil can be embedded into designs. Foil also looks good stuck to the back of a painted design in a card. Here is the same design shown three different ways, so that you can see the effects aluminium foil can have behind painted glass.

△ *This painted fish is laid on a piece of white paper.*

△ *Here a piece of crinkled foil, like the one shown right, has been put behind the fish.*

△ *This fish has a smooth piece of the dull side aluminium foil, like the one shown right, behind it.*

91 Using moulds

Use water-based paints (the thick creamy type that is transparent when dry), or gel paints in moulds. You can buy moulds in various designs – letters, sweets, animals, flowers, fruits etc – from kitchen shops, where they are sold for chocolate work, or from craft shops. Make letters and stick them onto glass items to spell out names or messages. When you want to change the message, store redundant letters on a sheet of glass until they are needed again.

1 Squeeze the thick water-based paint into the mould and leave it to dry. if it looks a little thin, add another layer.
2 When dry, ease the letter out of the mould – the tip of a craft knife can be helpful here.
3 Trim off any excess paint round the edges with scissors.

1

2

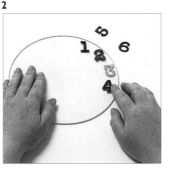

3

You can make an instant clock by sticking letters around a circle of glass and then fitting hands and a motion.

SAFETY WITH CHILDREN
If you have children, don't leave filled moulds within reach. The contents often look like sweets and children may be tempted to eat them.

FILLING DEEP MOULDS
If you are using a shallow mould, fill it with paint and let it dry. If your mould is deep, like this leaf mould, put one thin layer of paint in and let it dry, then keep adding layers of paint until you get the depth you want. If you fill the mould in one go, the paint will dry on top but will be wet underneath and the shape will be impossible to get out.

92 Using metal leaf

Metal leaf is easy to use and it can lend a wonderfully sumptuous look to painted designs. It is available in a range of colours and finishes. Leaf can be used in a number of ways, but here are the two techniques we use most often.

Metal leafing a large area

1 Using pipe-and-peel outliner, outline a design onto glass in the usual way (see 2 How to outline, page 19) and leave it to dry.

2 Paint a thin layer of acrylic size over the glass and outliner and leave it for five to ten minutes to go tacky.

3 Gently lay the leaf onto the glass. It is very fragile, so take care. However, if it does break, you can always patch it with extra bits and it won't show.

4 With a soft brush, gently brush the gold down onto the glass.

5 Use a stiffer brush to push the leaf right into all the corners of the outlined design.

6 Using a craft knife, trim off any excess leaf around the edges of the glass.

7 Use a craft knife to carefully lift a corner of the outliner and then gently pull all the outliner off the glass.

8 Paint over the leaf with shellac varnish and leave it to dry.

1

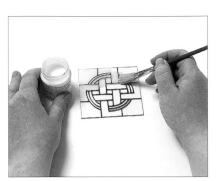

2

3

4

5

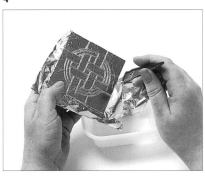

6

7

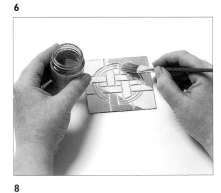

8

RECYCLING METAL LEAF
Keep any scraps of metal leaf in a sealed container to use on small areas or for patching torn leaf.

Metal leafing small areas

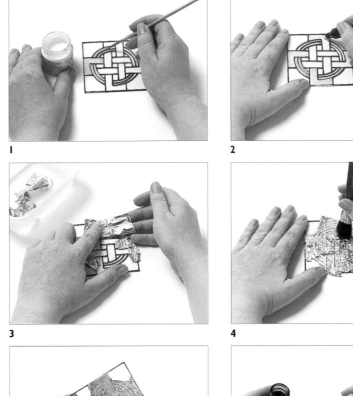

1 Outline a design onto glass (see 2 How to outline, page 19) and leave it to dry. Use a fine brush to paint areas of the design with acrylic size.

2 Alternatively use a special size pen to fill in the areas to be leafed.

3 Lay scraps of metal leaf onto the sized glass. Don't worry if it extends beyond the sized areas; any excess will be brushed off later.

4 Use a stiff brush to push the leaf into the corners of the sized areas,

5 Brush off any excess leaf

6 Paint the bare areas of glass with transparent paints.

△ *Silver leaf within a piped silver outline, surrounded by blue paint.*

△ *Gold leaf over black under-outlining that has been left in place.*

△ *Pink-toned copper leaf on the back of the glass, with areas painted in transparent paints on the front.*

△ *This sample was done in exactly the same way as the large design illustrated opposite, but we used pink-toned copper leaf instead.*

93 Making flowers with wire and paint

You can have some fun with this three-dimensional technique and children in particular will love it. Use pipe-and-peel water-based paints and silver fuse wire and florist's wire in varying thicknesses, depending on how big a petal or leaf you want to make. The florist's wire is available in pre-cut lengths that are easy to use.

▷ *Arrange flowers and leaves in a vase for an everlasting display.*

1

2

4

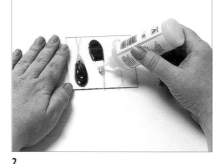

5

6

1 To make petals, take a piece of wire and curve it in half. Twist the ends together about two-thirds of the way down to make a petal shape.

2 Lay several petal wire shapes flat on a piece of glass and fill them in with paint, mixing the colours as you go and ensuring that you cover the wire.

3 When dry, the petals will peel off the glass – though they may need help from a craft knife to get started.

4 To make leaves, lay a thicker, straight piece of wire on the glass and, using green paint, draw an outline round it in the shape of a leaf.

USING SILVER WIRE

Use fuse and florist's wire with a silver finish, as it will disappear into the paint more easily.

---

5 Then fill in the outline, making sure you cover the wire well. When the leaf is dry, peel it off the glass and bend it into any position you want.

6 You can even embed some glass beads into clear-drying paint to make dew-covered leaves. Make them in the same way as the petals.

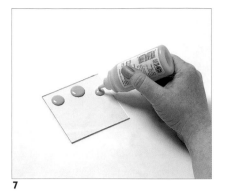

7

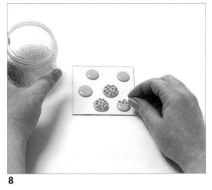

8

9

7 To make the stems and centres of the flowers, squeeze blobs of yellow paint onto the glass.

8 Sprinkle some glass beads onto the paint and leave it to dry.

9 Lift the beaded blobs of paint off the glass. You may need a craft knife to lift them off cleanly

10 Squeeze the malleable paint to make the flat blob into a cup shape. Make a small loop in the end of a length of thicker wire (which will be the stem) and fit it into the cup.

11 Squeeze a small amount of clear drying paint into the cup to hold the loop in place.

12 Stand the flower centres in a bottle while the clear paint dries.

13 Take your first petal and position it beside a flower centre. Wrap the loose ends of the wire around the stem, just under the yellow centre.

14 Work your way round the flower centre adding petals. If you keep the petals standing upright you will find this easier to do.

15 When all the petals are in place, wrap a strip of green florist's tape tightly around the top of the stem.

16 Add a dew-covered leaf to the stem, by wrapping the ends of the wire round the stem, then wrapping the tape over the wire and down to the bottom of the stem.

17 Curl the petals out around the centre of the flower.

10

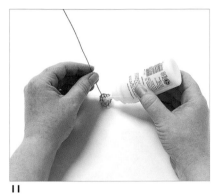

11

12

13

14

15

16

17

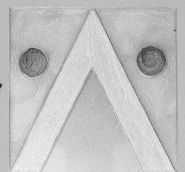
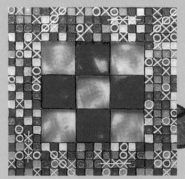

projects

We have incorporated many of the techniques from the first part of this book into this project section. Each project is illustrated with clear step-by-step photographs and we have included helpful tips, as well as alternative ideas for some of the designs. Also, every one of the designs used is given in the Motif Library, along with many others.

We have listed the colours and types of paints we used for each project, but, of course, you can vary these to make the project suit the room you want to display it in, or the taste of the person you are making it for. Whatever colours you use, always plan the picture first and paint the glass in the right sequence: dark colours first, then light colours. Always paint in this order, as if you accidentally drop a spot of a dark colour into a light one, it will really show and it is difficult to remove completely. However, if you drop a light colour into a dark one, it can just be lifted out with a clean brush and the residue won't show.

The projects vary in terms of the skills needed to make them, from the key cupboard to the layered picture frame, which you really must practise for. Always work within your skill level when tackling projects: start with easy ones and move on to more difficult ones. We hope that you will want to make many of the projects shown and that you will also be inspired by them to develop your own ideas.

1 Honey-bee key cupboard

From this key cupboard you can see that you don't have to have light shining through glass for it to look good. You can stick the glass straight onto a plain wooden door, though, if you are painting the cupboard, paint the section behind the glass white, or the colours of the glass paints you use will be distorted. You can use exactly the same method to make a panel for a kitchen or bathroom cabinet door, though as it may get wet or greasy, paint the design onto the back of the glass and stick the painted side to the cupboard to protect it.

MATERIALS

Key cupboard

Sheet of 2mm- (¹/₁₆in-) thick glass cut to fit the door. (This should not be too tight a fit or you may break it when fitting it.)

Epoxy glue

Honey-bee key cupboard template, page 140

Black outliner

Fine brush

White solvent-based pearl paint

Brown, orange, yellow, amber, clear and black solvent-based transparent paints

TECHNIQUES

2 How to outline, page 19

37 Solvent-based pearl paints, page 42

38 Solvent-based transparent paints, page 43

66 Using epoxy glue, page 62

MORE IDEAS

We crackle-glazed the honey-bee cupboard but, for a more country-style design, a plain pine cupboard is perfect. Give it two coats of matt varnish to seal the wood before gluing the glass in position.

1

2

3

4

5

6

1 Enlarge the template to the size you require. Outline the design onto the glass and leave it to dry. Paint the bees in sections, starting with the stripes. We used brown rather than harsh black, alternated with bands of combined yellow and orange. Remember to let the brown stripes dry before painting the yellow ones.

2 Paint the bees' legs black.

3 We used white pearl paint for the wings.

4 Paint the honeycomb with amber and yellow transparent paints and add a drop of clear paint to the centre of each hexagon. When you have finished painting, let the piece dry completely.

5 Put blobs of epoxy glue on the back of the bees' wings. they won't show through the pearl paint.

6 Carefully place the glass into the cupboard door.

ATTACHING THE GLASS

An alternative way sticking the glass in place is to run a line of outliner around the edge, between the glass and the wood.

2 Celestial mobile

A mobile can be made from glass, plastic or thick film and can be painted using almost any of the techniques in this book, as long as it is suitable for the base material you choose. We have made this heavenly mobile from light-weight, thick film and painted it with acrylic glass and solvent-based pearl paints.

MATERIALS

Moon, sun, rainbow and star templates, page 141

Thick film

White solvent-based pearl paint

Peach, blue, violet, light orange, deep orange, yellow, clear, turquoise, green and red acrylic glass paints

Fine brush

Silver outliner

Metal scouring pad

Scissors

Cutting mat

Bradawl

Fine florist's wire

Thin silver wool

Heavy florist's wire

Pin-nosed pliers

TECHNIQUES

1

2

4

3

5

1 Enlarge the templates to the required sizes. You will need one moon (ours measures 13.5cm [5¼in] across), five stars of varying sizes (ours measure from 6cm [2½in] to 3.5cm [1⅜in] across), two suns (ours measure 10cm [4in] across), and two rainbows (ours measure 14.5cm [5¾in] across the bottom of the arch). Outline the designs onto the film and leave them to dry. Paint the moon with white pearl paint, with circles of peach acrylic glass paint for the cheeks, added after the white pearl paint has dried. The star is painted with light orange and yellow acrylic glass paints. The background sky is painted with blue, violet and clear acrylic glass paints.

2 When the paint is dry, add tiny 'stars' to the sky, made from of blobs of silver outliner.

3 Paint the sun in deep orange, yellow and clear acrylic glass paints, with bright turquoise for the eyes. The rainbow is simply painted in the appropriate-coloured stripes of acrylic glass paint.

4 When all the painted pieces are dry, cut them out with either scissors, a craft knife or a hot stencil cutter.

5 Using a cutting mat to protect your worksurface, make a small hole in the top of each piece of the mobile with a bradawl or the tip of a compass.

6 Thread up each piece of the mobile. Use fairly long pieces of wool initially, as they can be adjusted once the mobile is hanging. Take a small piece of fine florist's wire and bend it in half. Put one end of the thin silver wool through the loop then push the wire through the hole in the mobile piece and pull the thread through. Tie the ends in a knot.

STOPPING THE MOBILE PIECES BENDING

If you want to use a paint that takes a few days to dry, you may find that as it dries it shrinks and bends the film a little. To counteract this, when your mobile is finished run a line of outliner around the outside of the piece, on the back, and paint the back with clear paint. This will stop it bending.

6

7

8

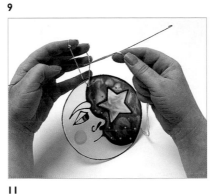

9

10

11

12

7 One way to add a bit of twinkle to the stars is to embed slivers of metal into the paint. Buy a gold or silver scouring pad and cut it into tiny bits.

8 Paint the stars with clear or yellow acrylic glass paint, then just sprinkle the bits of gold scouring pad into the wet paint and leave it to dry.

9 Thread up two of the large stars as above. Make the other three into a chain with the largest star at the top and the smallest at the bottom. Thread each star onto a strand of wool and tie knots in the wool to keep them spaced out.

10 Cut one 35cm (14in) length of heavy florist's wire and two 18cm (7in) lengths. Using the pin-nosed pliers, bend a small loop at each end of each piece.

11 Tie a length of silver wool to the centre of the long piece of heavy wire to hang the mobile from. Loop the length of wool holding the moon over the hanging length so that the moon hangs from the centre of the long piece of wire.

12 Attach a hanging length to the centre of each shorter piece of wire and loop a star over it. Hook a sun and a rainbow on the small loops at each end of each shorter piece of wire. Then hook the hanging lengths of the shorter pieces on the loops at the ends of the long piece of wire. Your mobile is now complete, but you will probably need to adjust the lengths of the pieces of wool to get it to hang correctly. In our experience it either

hangs perfectly the first time or we spend ages fiddling about with it. One tip that may help you is to try to keep the smaller pieces approximately the same size and weight. You can also alter the balance of the mobile by adjusting the central threads along the wire.

CHOOSING THE RIGHT
WEIGHT OF WIRE
When making the mobiles, the thick film only needs heavy florist's wire to hang it from. Plastic will need a slightly thicker wire and if you are making a glass mobile, use cut-up wire coat hangers to suspend the pieces from.

3 Modern mirror tiles

Making your own mirror and glass tiles is great because you can create so many designs and make various projects from them afterwards. Take a piece of fabric or wallpaper and make tiles to match: just as with interior design, the possibilities are endless. Leave some sections of the design blank when you are painting it so that the mirror backing shows through.

MATERIALS

Squares of 3mm- (⅛in-) thick plain glass cut to the size you require

Squares of 3mm- (⅛in-) thick mirror glass cut to the same size as the plain glass

Tile templates, page 141

Silver outliner

Cream, pink, white, purple, turquoise, light green and yellow pearl paints

Fine brush

Silicone glue

One index finger (to spread the silicone glue with)

TECHNIQUES

2 How to outline, page 19

37 Solvent-based pearl paints, page 42

67 Using silicone glue, page 63

BACKING THE TILES

Don't be tempted to put the tiles straight onto the walls without a mirror backing, as the grouting or plaster can lift the paint off the glass as it dries.

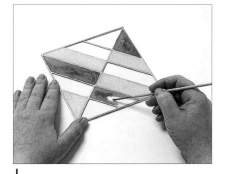

1

2

3

4

1 Enlarge the templates to the size you require. Outline the designs onto the plain glass squares with silver outliner and leave them to dry. Paint sections of the tiles with a mix of cream, pink and white pearl paints. Paint other sections with a mix of turquoise, purple and white.
2 Finally, paint sections with a mix of light green, yellow and white pearl

paints. Leave some sections blank so that the mirror backing will show through. Leave the tiles to dry completely for a few days.
3 Place each square of painted glass face down onto a piece of mirror. Run a thin line of silicone glue around the join between the glass and mirror.
4 Smooth the glue into the edge of the tile with your finger and let it dry.

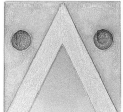
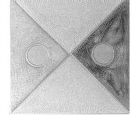

◁ △ *Use these pictures to guide you when painting the tiles.*

MORE IDEAS

You can back the tiles with various things to protect them. Use plain or textured glass if you want the tiles to be see-through, for a room divider for example. A mirror-glass backing reflects light, while using a white ceramic tile to back a glass tile gives a flat, even background to your design.

△ *This design is backed with a white ceramic tile.*

△ *Here is the same design, but this time backed with mirror glass.*

4 Decorated light bulbs

Painted light bulbs can totally transform a room and add character and atmosphere, yet they are very simple and inexpensive to make.

We tend to work on 15- to 40-watt clear bulbs; pearl bulbs diffuse the image too much. We just make simple designs on the bulbs, as they won't last forever. Shown here are two of our favourite techniques for decorating light bulbs.

▷ *The pattern from a pipe-and-peel harlequin bulb is reflected onto the lampshade when the light is turned on.*

Rainbow light bulb

We like to paint the colours on in the accepted order; red, orange, yellow, green, blue and violet, from the top to bottom of the bulb.

MATERIALS

Light bulb

Wire

Red, orange, yellow, green, blue and violet light bulb paints

Fine brush

Gold outliner

TECHNIQUES

2 How to outline, page 19

44 Light bulb paints, page 49

1

2

1 Before you start painting, wrap a length of wire around the end of the bulb and bend it into a hook. This allows you to hang the bulb up to dry.

2 Paint three rings of colour: one near the bayonet end, one in the middle and one at the top in blue, yellow and red respectively. Hang the bulb up until the paint is dry.

3 Then paint in the other three rings of colour, starting next to the bayonet, in violet, green and orange respectively. It doesn't matter if the colours overlap a little. Hang the bulb up to dry.

4 You can leave the bulb just like this, or you can outline some zodiac symbols onto the bulb in gold outliner.

3

4

DRYING BULBS

A mug tree is useful for hanging your light bulbs on to dry.

Patterned light bulb

You can outline designs straight onto the bulb, but we find the pipe-and-peel technique the best to use.

MATERIALS

Light bulb

Wire

Black pipe-and-peel outliner

Fish template, page 141

Red, yellow, blue and violet light bulb paints

Fine brush

TECHNIQUES

8 Pipe-and-peel outlining, page 22

44 Light bulb paints, page 49

1

2

3

1 Wire your bulb, as described left. Pipe your designs (we used a fish) onto a piece of glass and leave to dry. Peel the fish off the glass and stick them onto the bulb.

2 Paint the first colours: we combined red and yellow in the fins and head. Hang the bulb up to dry.

3 Paint the rest of the body, one colour at a time. We painted it half blue and half violet. Hang the bulb up to dry.

OUTLINING ONTO BULBS

You can use a combination of outlining techniques on light bulbs. Pipe-and-peel flowers and stick them to the light bulb. Then outline simple leaves straight onto the bulb to join all the flowers together.

5 Contemporary painted table

You can convert an inexpensive glass-topped table into a work of art. We chose a circular table, as the shape suited the design we wanted to use, but you can choose another design and make a rectangular or square coffee table using the same method. We once made a three-dimensional coffee table with a shoal of Koi carp swimming through it, and a large glass-topped dining table, with painted plates and glasses to match. Positioning a light underneath can look stunning, but don't go too mad or all the colour may put you off your food.

As tables get a lot of wear and tear, we usually paint the underside of the glass. So remember that your design will be reversed when it is finished. If you want to use the painted side, protect it with a piece of glass on top or a few coats of tough varnish.

MATERIALS

Round, glass-topped table

Table template, page 140

Black, gold and silver outliner

Royal blue, turquoise, white, amber and brown solvent-based pearl paints

Fine brush

Clear pipe-and-peel paint

TECHNIQUES

2 How to outline, page 19

37 Solvent-based pearl paints, page 42

41 Pipe-and-peel paints, page 46

1 Firstly, dismantle the table. Enlarge the template to fit the table top – you may have to do this on several pieces of paper and tape them together. Outline the design onto the glass and leave it to dry. Pipe dots of silver and gold outliner around the narrow lines in the design.

2 Plan the order you are going to paint the glass in. This is important when painting a large area or you will get ridges where the edge of the paint dried before you got back to it. The best method is to paint a short distance in one direction, then a short distance in another direction. Continue painting like this until the edges meet. We painted this section in turquoise, royal blue and white pearl paints.

3 Paint some of the thin lines (painting over the dots of gold and silver outliner) in amber and white pearl paints.

4 Paint the remaining thin lines in brown and white pearl paint. When all the pearl paint is dry, scribble clear pipe-and peel paint onto the areas of unpainted glass.

SAFETY WITH GLASS

The glass that comes with the table will be suitable for the purpose, but if you are having a piece of glass cut, check the safety requirements and, especially for a large table, consider using toughened glass.

1

2

3

4

6 Koi carp vase

One of the most relaxing things in the world must be watching Koi carp swim. I find the way they move around the water like a living piece of art fascinating. With those fantastic colours, the carp makes the drabbest pond look great. To keep the association with water, we put this Koi carp onto a vase.

MATERIALS

Vase

Self-adhesive film

Koi carp template, page 141

Black outliner

Black, orange and white solvent-based pearl paints

White iridescent paint

Fine brush

TECHNIQUES

2 How to outline, page 19

37 Solvent based pearl paints, page 42

50 Iridescent paints, page 52

69 Self-adhesive film, page 64

◁ You can paint these fish in many colour combinations. For more fish designs, use the alternative Koi template on page 141 and the fish in the templates for the three-dimensional Koi carp picture on page 156.

1 Photocopy the Koi carp template to the size you require. Lay a sheet of self-adhesive film over the template and outline the design onto the film, then leave it to dry.

2 Paint in the areas of black.

3 Next, paint in the orange areas.

4 Paint in all the white areas.

5 Scatter drops of iridescent white paint over the whole fish. These drops will blend in and help create a scaly look on the fish.

6 When the paint is dry, cut out the fish following the line of outliner.

7 Peel away the backing of the film and stick the fish onto the vase.

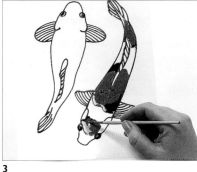

1

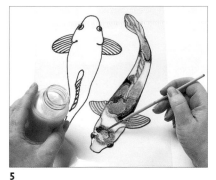

2

3

4

5

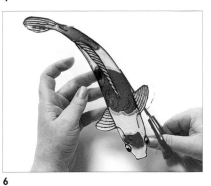

6

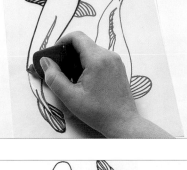

7

MAKING A LOT OF FISH

If you want to make lots of fish, use self-adhesive photocopy film. Outline the larger areas of the fish but not the details. If you have outlined all the detail, but have then painted over it, you can wait until everything is dry and then over-outline areas to bring out the detail again.

7 Letter bottles

These are fun to make. You can buy small bottles or collect them as you go along. Make a collection of lettered bottles so that you can spell out whatever you want; Happy Birthday, or, I love you, for example.

You can outline directly onto the glass, if you can get the template inside the bottle, or you could use the pipe-and peel technique. However, we find using self-adhesive film easiest.

MATERIALS

Glass bottles

Self-adhesive film

Alphabet template, page 142

Purple and pink solvent-based pearl paints

Kelly green and light green solvent-based transparent paints

Fine brush

Scissors

TECHNIQUES

2 How to outline, page 19

37 Solvent-based pearl paints, page 42

38 Solvent-based transparent paints, page 43

69 Self-adhesive film, page 64

1 First choose the letters you want to use. Enlarge the templates to the size you require. Place your film over them, outline the letter and the surrounding box and leave them to dry. Paint the letters themselves first: we chose to paint them with a combination of purple and pink pearl paints.

2 When the letters are dry, paint the box backgrounds. We used kelly green transparent paint, fading into light green transparent paint. Leave to dry completely.

3 Carefully cut out the letters with a pair of sharp scissors.

4 Peel the backing off the film and stick each letter to a bottle.

1

2

3

4

MORE IDEAS

The letters on page 142 can be painted using almost any of the techniques shown in this book. Here is a whole alphabet of examples to inspire you. We have listed the techniques we used, but do experiment and dream up your own combinations.

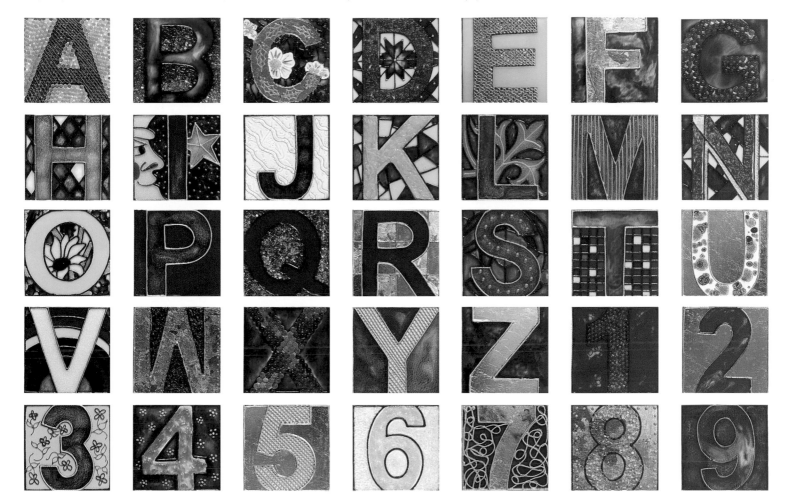

A layered gel paint and embedding.

B solvent-based transparent paints and embedding.

C solvent-based pearl and transparent paints and gold paint.

D gel and solvent-based transparent paints.

E layered gel, gold and opaque paints.

F metal leaf and solvent-based transparent paints

G embedding and solvent-based transparent paints.

H solvent-based pearl paints with gold over-outlining.

I solvent-based pearl and transparent paints with gold and silver over-outlining.

J solvent-based pearl paints and textured paint with gold over-outlining.

K gel and solvent-based transparent paints.

L solvent-based pearl and transparent paints with gold over-outlining.

M solvent-based pearl and transparent paints with silver over-outlining.

N iridescent gel and solvent-based transparent paints.

O solvent-based pearl and transparent paints.

P solvent-based pearl paints.

Q solvent-based transparent paints and embedding.

R solvent-based transparent paints with metal leaf and gold over-outlining.

S solvent-based pearl paints with silver over-outlining.

T solvent-based transparent paints.

U opaque, solvent-based transparent paints and metal leaf.

V solvent-based transparent paints.

W metal leaf and gel paints.

X solvent-based transparent paints and embedding.

Y gold outliner and solvent-based pearl paints.

Z metal leaf and solvent-based transparent paints.

I solvent-based transparent paints and embedding

2 solvent-based transparent paints and metal leaf.

3 solvent-based pearl and transparent paints with gold over-outlining and pen work.

4 gel, solvent-based transparent paints and pen work.

5 layered outliner and metal leaf.

6 iridescent gel paints.

7 metal leaf and solvent-based transparent paint with gold over-outlining.

8 gel paint and gold outlining with metal leaf.

9 solvent-based pearl paints and silver over-outlining.

*Those of you looking for a nought, we always use the **O** from the alphabet.*

8 Mosaic vase

You can have lots of fun with this project. Make the simple vase shown and put either
flowers or a candle into it. Once the film has been painted, this is an ideal project for
children, as it really doesn't matter if the mosaic 'tiles' are not perfectly square.

MATERIALS

Vase

Mosaic tile template, page 144

Coloured pencils

Cloth

Self-adhesive film

Fine brush

Scissors

Royal blue, purple, clear, kelly green, light green, yellow, orange and red solvent-based transparent paints

Gold outliner

TECHNIQUES

69 Using self-adhesive film, page 64

88 Making mosaic, page 79

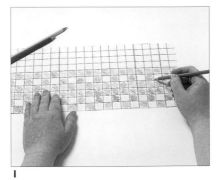

1

2

3

4

5

1 We like to make a plan before we start making mosaics. Photocopy the template to fit your vase: you may need to enlarge it and tape several copies together. Then compose your design by colouring in the squares with pencils. We have made a very simple design of alternating coloured squares, but, of course, you can make any pattern you choose.

2 Curl up the template and fit it into the vase. Push a cloth into the middle to press the template up against the vase. This makes it much easier to work on as you can see exactly where the 'tiles' should be placed.

3 Paint the film to match the coloured squares on the template. We used gold outliner on two of the colours as it gives another dimension to the 'tiles'. Cut the painted film up into 'tiles' approximately the same size as the squares on the template.

4 Starting at the top of the vase, peel the backing off the film and stick the 'tiles' onto the glass over the appropriate-coloured squares. You can always trim the 'tiles' a little if they are too big.

5 Work round and down the vase, following the template, until you get to the bottom.

9 Noughts and crosses board

We were once challenged to make something attractive to look at, practical and fun to use and yet simple to make, all from a flat piece of glass. Our answer was this noughts and crosses board. You can hang it in the window or on a wall and it looks like a piece of art, or you can put it on the table and play a game of noughts and crosses; or black grapes and green grapes, glass dolphins and fish, the combinations are endless. So long as you have five of each object, you can play a noughts and crosses-style game.

We painted this board with a mixture of pearl and translucent paints and over-outlined it with gold outliner. However, the decorative possibilities are as limitless as your imagination, so do experiment.

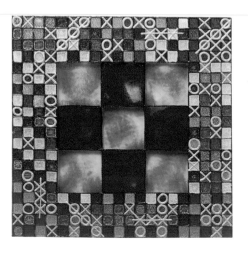

MATERIALS

Board and pieces templates, page 144

Square of 4mm- (³⁄₁₆in-) thick glass cut to fit board template

Ten squares of 4mm- (³⁄₁₆in-) thick glass cut to fit pieces templates

Black and gold outliner

Red, flame orange, light orange, yellow and clear solvent-based transparent paints

Red, purple, yellow, green, royal blue and turquoise solvent-based pearl paints

Fine brush

TECHNIQUES

2 How to outline, page 19

4 Over-outlining, page 20

37 Solvent-based pearl paints, page 42

38 Solvent-based transparent paints, page 43

58 Cutting straight lines in glass, page 58

1 Enlarge the board template to the required size and outline the design onto the large square of glass. Leave it to dry.

2 Working on the border first, paint in squares, either randomly or in a pattern, with pearl paints. Paint a few squares, not ones adjacent to one another, then add a drop of white to each one. Continue painting in this way, allowing squares to dry before painting the ones next to them.

3 When the border is dry, paint the middle squares with translucent paints, combining red and flame orange in half of them and yellow and light orange in the other half. Add a few drops of clear paint to each square.

4 When all the paint is dry, over-outline the border with noughts and crosses in gold outliner. You can do this randomly or actually have little games with yourself all the way around the board.

5 When everything is completely dry, stick a small plastic bubble foot to the back of each corner to protect the board and any furniture you intend to put it on. This also makes it easier to pick up.

6 Outline the border round the edge of each of the small glass squares. You can do this freehand or lay them over the pieces templates. Leave them to dry.

7 Using pearl paints, paint five pieces green and five red. When the paint is dry, over-outline noughts onto the red squares and crosses onto the green ones.

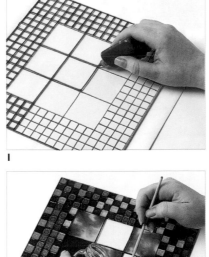

1

2

3

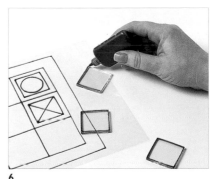

4

5

6

7

DRYING TIMES

Always let your projects dry completely. The time needed will depend on the paints, but if you leave the pieces on the board before it is fully dry, they may stick to it and damage the paint.

MORE IDEAS

A simpler board can be made without a border. For quick and easy game pieces, either pipe glass mosaic squares or use sets of small objects: on this board the dolphins have just beaten the fish. For a compact game set, pipe the noughts and crosses board onto the lid of a small glass box and keep all your game pieces inside the box. Glass shapes or piped glass nuggets make good pieces.

You can also make boards and pieces for chess (pipe each square with a picture or letter), draughts, backgammon and if you have the patience, Scrabble.

10 Ocean aquarium

Whenever possible we try to have a bit of fun with our glass painting. Alan suggested that we put fish swimming round this aquarium. Barry suggested adding a diver. Alan then suggested a shark, creeping up on the diver. So we used all three elements in the design. We turned the finished tank round, so that the design is seen through the water and behind the goldfish in the tank. Instead of gravel we used glass beads, nuggets and shapes to decorate the tank floor.

MATERIALS

Glass fish tank

Ocean aquarium motifs, page 144

Outliner

Red, yellow, peach, cerise, turquoise, clear and purple solvent-based transparent paints

Royal blue, turquoise, white and black solvent-based pearl paints

Silver artist's acrylic paint

Fine brush

TECHNIQUES

2 How to outline, page 19

37 Solvent-based pearl paints, page 42

38 Solvent-based transparent paints, page 43

49 Artist's acrylic paints, page 52

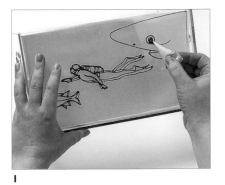

1

2

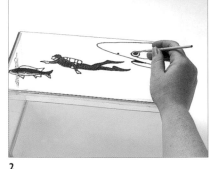

3

1 Enlarge the design to fit your fish tank and tape it to the inside of the glass. Outline the design and let it dry. If you want to paint all four sides of the tank, do the front and a side section first, let them dry and then do the back and the other side.

2 When the outliner is dry, paint one side of the tank at a time, not moving on to the next side until the paint is completely dry. Because this project will be used with water, we used solvent-based paints.

3 We painted the shark and diver mainly in pearl paints, using transparent paints for the eye, face, hands and aqualung straps and silver artist's acrylic paint for the aqualung itself. We painted the small fish in transparent paints.

CREATING BUBBLES

If you wish you can also squeeze little blobs of clear, textured paint onto the glass. When they dry they will look like air bubbles.

MAKING A FISH TANK

You can either buy a fish tank or make your own using waterproof silicone glue. Cut the pieces of glass to size, paint them first then and stick them together in the same way as the Gilded Box on page 130.

If you decide to buy a fish tank, as we did, open the box and look at it before you make the purchase. We didn't do this and our tank turned out to be a badly made affair. It took longer to clean it up and make it presentable than it would have done to make our own.

11 Sailing ships

A few ships hanging in a window can look very grand and relaxing and make an otherwise dull view more interesting. You can have just one ship or a whole harbour full.

Each ship template comes in two parts – a basic ship and one with the rigging, which is added after painting. Cut out the glass shape following the basic ship outline and drill two holes near the top if you want to hang the finished ship.

△ You can hang ships from nylon thread and it will look as though they are sailing through the air. Alternatively, cut a 3mm- (⅛in-) wide groove in a strip of wood and stand a ship in that. The wood can be varnished, or even given a coat of glass paint, which will stain the wood.

▽ You don't have to stick to traditional wood colours for the ship's hull. We used quite bright colours for this galleon.

MATERIALS

2mm- (¹/₁₆in-) thick glass

Ship templates, page 146

Glass cutter

Sanding pad

Drill

Black outliner

White solvent-based pearl paint

Amber and black solvent-based transparent paints

Fine brush

Gold pen

Nylon thread

TECHNIQUES

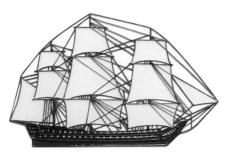

1

2

3

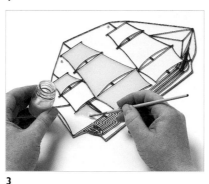

4

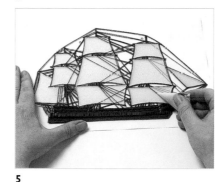

5

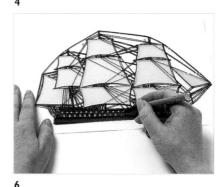

6

1 Place the glass ship shape on top of the basic ship template and outline the hull, masts and sails.

2 Mix your own antique white paint to give the sails an authentic canvas look. Add a few drops of amber transparent paint to white pearl paint to turn it off-white. Give the bottle a shake to mix the paint and then let it rest for a few minutes for the bubbles to disperse before you use it.

3 Paint the ship's sails; paint alternate sails and let them dry before painting the adjacent ones. Leave them to dry.

4 Then paint in the hull. We used bands of black and amber transparent paint, leaving it to dry in between colours.

5 When the paint is dry, place the ship over the rigging template and over-outline all the rigging. Leave it to dry.

6 Finally, add details and highlights with a gold pen or gold outliner.

USING SELF-ADHESIVE FILM FOR SHIPS

Pipe and paint the ships onto self-adhesive film and stick them directly onto your windows. Or, for another version of a traditional ship-in-a-bottle, stick the film to a clear glass bottle.

MORE IDEAS

We made the same style of ship on a larger scale, using self-adhesive brass and lead strip instead of ordinary outliner. We think that it looks most impressive.

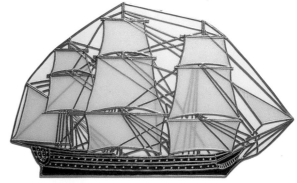

12 Potted trees

These fruit trees look great on a kitchen window sill or in a conservatory. During the day they will look bright and cheerful and at night the candles behind them will glow through the painted glass, giving a lovely warm light. They are not only decorative, but if you add a few drops of essential oil to the pots, they will make the room smell good as well and when the smell fades it can be easily refreshed by adding a few more drops of oil to the pots. Try using lemon oil on the lemon tree and orange oil on the orange tree for an authentic touch. You could make a Christmas tree by adding a partridge to the pear tree and using cinnamon oil to scent the tree.

SAFETY WITH CANDLES
Place candle and tree in a safe place and out of a draught. Never leave a lighted candle unattended and do not allow it to burn right down. The trees can also be made of plastic or thick film, though you cannot then add a candle, as the the flame will melt the plastic or film.

FILLING THE POT
You can also fill the pot with plaster, but this is done after painting. Possible problems are that you cannot remove the tree and, if you make the plaster too thick, as it dries it expands and may crack the pot. So, make the plaster thin and soak the pot in cold water before filling it.

◁ *Use pearl paints for lemons and oranges, but for smooth-skinned apples and pears, we use transparent paints. The motifs for all the fruit trees are on page 145.*

MATERIALS
Terracotta flower pot, 9cm (3½in) in diameter

Masking tape and air-drying clay

Glass strip for the trunk, 24cm x 3cm (9½in x 1¼in)

Florist's plastic candle-holder

Tree motif, page 145

Glass circle for the tree, 14cm (5½in) in diameter

Black outliner

Ultra-violet glue

Yellow and white solvent-based pearl paints

Dark green, light green, brown, amber and clear solvent-based transparent paints

Fine brush

Gravel or glass nuggets

TECHNIQUES
2 How to outline, page 19

37 Solvent-based pearl paints, page 42

38 Solvent-based transparent paints, page 43

58 Cutting straight lines in glass, page 58

60 Cutting glass circles, page 59

65 Using ultra-violet glue, page 62

1

3

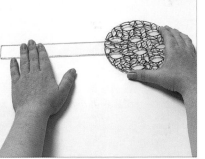

7

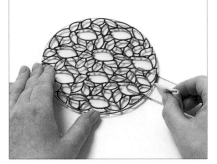

1

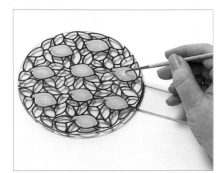

8

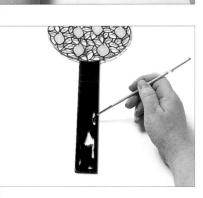

4

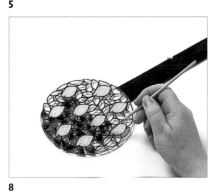

5

2

9

1 Stick a small piece of masking tape over the hole in the bottom of the pot and then fill the pot up with clay to about 1.5cm (½in) from the top.

2 Push the trunk into the soft clay, just off centre, right down to the bottom of the pot, then wriggle it about a bit. You need to do this to make the hole bigger than the trunk, as when the clay dries it shrinks, so the hole will be smaller and the trunk may not fit into it easily.

3 Push the candle-holder into the clay behind the trunk, making sure it is upright and not too close to the glass – you don't want the heat from the candle to crack it. Then remove the trunk and wash it ready for painting. Leave the clay to dry for at least a day.

4 Enlarge the tree template to fit the glass circle, outline the design onto it and leave it to dry. Using ultra-violet glue (though two-part epoxy glue or silicone are acceptable alternatives), stick the trunk to the centre back of the tree. Make sure that the fruit on the tree is hanging downwards or it will look rather odd.

5 To stop the paint running between the two pieces of glass, run a line of outliner along the join.

6 Now paint the lemons. We like to use yellow pearl paint, with a drop of white in the middle, as when the paint is dry it looks a bit like the dimpled skin of a lemon.

7 While the lemons are drying you can paint the trunk. Combine brown and amber transparent paints to get a wood effect. Leave to dry.

8 Lastly paint the leaves. You can achieve a more three-dimensional effect by painting half of each leaf in light green and the other half in dark green. Paint them a few at a time so that the colours flow together a little while the paints are wet.

9 Leave the paint to dry and harden for at least 24 hours, so that when you slip the trunk into the hole in the clay, the paint is not damaged. Sprinkle gravel, or glass nuggets, over the surface of the clay and put the candle in the holder behind the trunk. We tend to use a white candle at the back of the tree so that it doesn't distort the colours. You can use scented candles; again, choose a the scent to complement the fruit.

13 Mirrored candle sconce

We love the effect you get when using candles with painted glass, especially painted mirror glass. This sconce is designed to take tealights – not big, heavy candles. If you want to see more mirror in your finished sconce, you can make it up in the same way, but just paint the border and leave the central part unpainted.

The templates are all in proportion to one another, so just enlarge them all by the same amount to make a sconce the size you require.

MATERIALS

Mirrored candle sconce templates, five in total, enlarged to the required size, page 148

4mm- (³⁄₁₆in-) thick mirror glass cut to fit the main template with a hole drilled near the top

3mm- (¹⁄₈in-) thick plain glass, cut to fit the four smaller templates

9mm- (³⁄₈in-) wide self-adhesive lead

Carbon paper

Black outliner

Purple, light green and kelly green solvent-based transparent paints

Fine brush

Silicone glue

Plastic glass-painting granules

TECHNIQUES

2 How to outline, page 19

9 Transferring designs onto mirror glass, page 24

21 Using self-adhesive lead, page 32

38 Solvent-based transparent paints, page 43

60 Cutting glass circles, page 59

61 Cutting glass shapes, page 60

62 Drilling holes in glass, page 60

67 Using silicone glue, page 63

87 Embedding objects in paint, page 78

1 Wrap self adhesive-lead around the outside edges of the mirror glass, bending it over and sticking it to the surface of the glass (see Suncatcher, page 122 for more details). At the pointed ends, snip into the lead on either side so that it bends smoothly round the corners.

2 Transfer the design onto the mirror, outline it and leave to dry.

3 Wrap self-adhesive lead around the plain glass circle. Outline the designs onto all the pieces of plain glass and leave to dry. Then paint the purple sections on the plain and mirror glass. The circle has been designed to fit over a particular area of the main design (lay the circle on the mirror and you will be able to line them up), so paint the same sections of these two pieces the same colours.

4 Paint sections of the plain and mirror glass with light green paint and when that has dried, paint other sections with kelly green paint.

5 Use silicone glue to stick the rectangles of glass in position. Stick the largest rectangle across the narrowest part of the painted design, with the smaller ones touching it on each side, as shown. Leave them to dry.

6 Pipe silicone glue onto the top edges of the rectangles and stick the circle to them. Leave to dry.

7 Working in short sections, paint the border of the mirror with a combination of light and kelly green paint and embed a generous quantity of glass-painting plastic granules into it. Then drop more paint over the granules to secure them firmly.

1

2

4

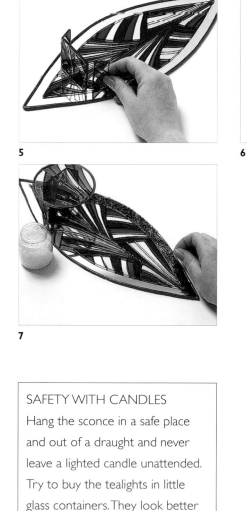

3

5

6

7

SAFETY WITH CANDLES
Hang the sconce in a safe place and out of a draught and never leave a lighted candle unattended. Try to buy the tealights in little glass containers. They look better when lit and the wax becomes clear as it melts.

MIRRORED CANDLE SCONCE **115**

14 Tile house number

This is a very unusual way to use a mirror and glass tile: set it in concrete or cement. Because the number will be on the back of the glass you need to use the reversed numeral templates, so that when you sandwich the glass and mirror together the number will be the right way round. We did not paint the number itself, so the mirror showing through will catch the light and the number will show up well.

MATERIALS

3mm- (⅛in-) thick glass square cut to size

3mm- (⅛in-) thick mirror glass square cut to the same size

Reversed numeral templates, page 143

Tile template, page 149

Black outliner

Royal blue, purple, white and amber solvent-based pearl paints

Fine brush

Silicone glue

Pizza box (without pizza)

Plastic parcel tape

Thin plastic film

Quick-drying cement

Trowel or palette knife

Sanding paper

Drill with bit to make holes in cement

TECHNIQUES

2 How to outline, page 19

3 Modern mirror tiles, page 94

37 Solvent-based pearl paints, page 42

58 Cutting straight lines in glass, page 58

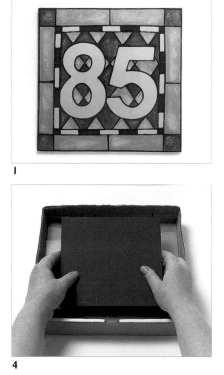

1

2

3

4

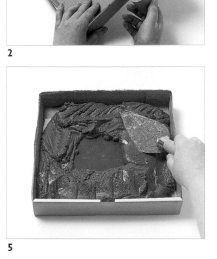

5

6

7

8

9

1 Make up a mirror tile as described in the *Modern mirror tiles* project. We painted this one in a blue and yellow colour scheme, but, of course, you can use whatever colours you want.

2 Take an ordinary pizza box and, using plastic parcel tape, tape up the outside of the box. If the box seems weak, tape the inside, too.

3 Lay some thin plastic film in the bottom of the box. This, and the tape, helps to stop the box from becoming soggy when you pour the cement in.

4 Place the tile face down in the box, making sure that it is in the centre.

5 Following the manufacturer's instructions, mix up the cement and trowel it over the tile. Trowel in a thin

layer around the edges of the tile first, making sure that you don't trap any air pockets and that the cement goes right to the corners. Take care not to move the tile.

6 Fill the box to the top with cement then use the trowel to smooth off the back.

MIXING THE CEMENT

Don't mix the cement up too wet, or it will saturate the box and distort it before it sets.

---

7 Leave the cement to dry for the recommended time. Then peel off the cardboard box and remove the plastic.

8 Use a boning tool or a knife to scrape away any excess cement on the front of the tile, taking care not to scratch it.

9 You can use sandpaper and a wire brush to smooth the edges of the cement. Drill a hole in each of the top corners of the cement and screw the number to your front wall.

REVERSING A DESIGN

If you have difficulty designing your house number or lettering backwards, just design it the right way round and photocopy it onto acetate, which you can then turn over and use as a template.

---

15 Etched coasters

The idea behind these coasters was to do two designs, one on each side of the glass, so they create an overlapping, three-dimensional effect. Display them on a coffee table, laid out like a picture, then you can use three or four together to put the coffee pot on and one or two to put the mugs on. When you have finished, reassemble the picture.

We used 4mm- (³⁄₁₆in-) thick glass, cut into 10cm (4in) squares for these coasters. This thickness is fine for everyday use, but if you need stronger glass use 6mm (³⁄₁₆in), or ask your glazier to toughen glass for you.

MATERIALS

Six 10cm (4in) squares of 4mm- (³⁄₁₆in-) thick glass

Top and bottom coaster templates, page 149

Peel-off outliner

Etching cream

Fine brush

Twenty-four small plastic bubble feet

TECHNIQUES

2 How to outline, page 19

58 Cutting straight lines in glass, page 58

71 Peel-off outliner as an etching mask, page 67

1 Enlarge the design for the top of the coasters to the required size. One at a time, lay a glass square over each section of the design in turn, outline the area and let it dry.

2 When you have outlined all the squares, they should look like this.

3 Following the safety instructions for the etching cream that you are using, paint the cream onto the areas that you want etched. Paint two or three squares at a time.

4 Wash off all the etching cream, remove all the outliner and dry the glass. You may find a craft knife useful for lifting off small pieces of outliner.

5 Enlarge the design for the bottom of the coasters to the required size. One at a time, lay the etched squares, etched side down, over a section of the design and outline the area. Make sure you get the squares in the right positions. Repeat the etching process as in steps 3 and 4.

6 When the coasters are finished, stick some small plastic bubble feet onto the bottom of each one to protect the surface of your table.

1

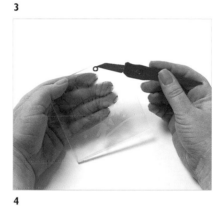
3

4

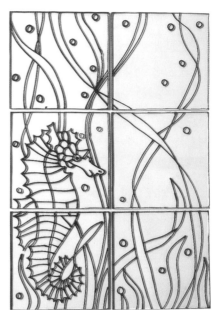
2

5

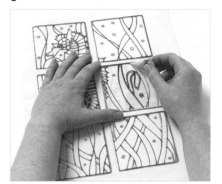
6

MORE IDEAS

You can also paint coasters. They look good with the top painted in transparent paints and the bottom in opaque paints. However, you must use a heat-resistant paint on the tops or the heat from the coffee cups will damage your design. Also, don't use outliner on the tops of the coasters as it will create an uneven surface and your cups will wobble. If you want to outline, do it on the back.

You can also just paint one side of the glass. This coaster was under-outlined in gold on the back, then painted in solvent-based transparent paints. This way the paint is protected under the glass and you have a nice smooth flat surface on top.

The coaster designs can also be made bigger, say 20cm (8in) square and used as table place mats. You could even make the coasters to match. The possibilities and combinations are endless.

PAINTING ON ETCHING CREAM

Don't be tempted to paint the etching cream onto all the pieces of glass at once, because you must wash off the cream at the manufacturer's recommended time. If you don't, the fumes the cream gives off will start to etch the uncovered glass and when you wash the cream off there will be an etched ghosting effect on the glass. However, if you want this effect, leave the cream on longer than recommended.

16 Art Deco clock

This exuberant Art Deco-style clock has extra glass pieces attached onto and underneath the central disc. This is a project where you can go to town with colour, so it is perfect for solvent-based pearl paints. Combine colours freely, letting them flow into one another to create interesting effects. The templates for the clock pieces are all in proportion to each other, so enlarge them all by the same amount. Drill a hole into the middle of the main circle large enough to take the clock motion, which you can get from many craft suppliers. The central part of the clock is made from 4mm- (³/₁₆in-) thick glass, so make sure that you buy a motion that will fit it.

MATERIALS

Circle of 4mm- (³/₁₆in-) thick glass the required diameter

Sheet of 2mm- (¹/₁₆in-) thick glass

Clock templates, page 150

Black outliner

Cerise, pink, amber, cream, white, royal blue, turquoise, kelly green, light green, purple, red and yellow solvent-based pearl paints

Fine brush

Epoxy glue

Clock motion with hands

TECHNIQUES

2 How to outline, page 19

37 Solvent-based pearl paints, page 42

58 Cutting straight lines in glass, page 58

60 Cutting glass circles, page 59

61 Cutting glass shapes, page 60

62 Drilling holes in glass, page 60

66 Using epoxy glue, page 62

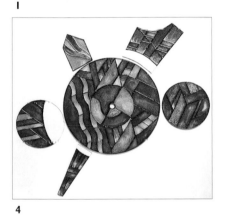

1

2

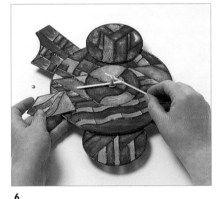

3

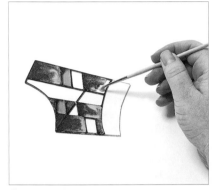

4

5

6

1 Paint the separate pieces of the clock with pearl paints. We have painted the various sections with different colour themes. This section is primarily pinks and blues.

2 Continue building up the colours but remember not to paint adjacent sections at the same time. Leave the areas marked on the templates with a dotted line un-painted. These areas will be glued to the back of the clock.

3 Don't be afraid to use vibrant colour combinations on different parts of the clock. The more multi-coloured this project is, the better.

4 When you have finished painting, let all the clock pieces dry completely.

Lay out all the painted sections of the clock in the arrangement they will go together in before you start to assemble it

5 Turn the central part of the clock upside down and, using clear epoxy glue, stick the unpainted areas on some of the clock sections to the back. When the glue is dry turn the clock over, then stick the remaining sections to the front of the clock. Leave the clock to dry.

6 Following the manufacturer's instructions, fit the clock motion.

17 Suncatcher

This project takes the ordinary painted suncatcher a step further. It uses two pieces of glass, instead of the normal one, with a photocopied piece of acetate or film in between. The photocopied design is then over-outlined and painted on the back of the suncatcher, so that the detail stands out clearly.

This method enables you to work with very detailed images easily, as you just have to outline the bolder lines. For example, it makes doing eye-catching, but rather eye-crossing, Celtic designs much easier. After a bit of practice you will be using photos, old prints, engravings: the possibilities are endless.

Photocopying is also good if you have to do lots of lettering on glass. Do the lettering on a computer, print it out and photocopy it onto acetate.

Alternatively, you can photocopy a design onto self-adhesive film, stick it to a circle of glass and make up the suncatcher with just that one circle. Outline and paint the back of the design in the same way as described in this project.

MATERIALS

Two circles of 2mm- (¹/₁₆in-) thick glass the size you want the finished suncatcher to be

Photocopy film

Suncatcher template, page 149

Pen

Paper

Scissors

Length of 9mm- (³/₈in-) wide brass-coloured, flat self-adhesive lead, the circumference of a glass circle, plus 5cm (2in)

Bradawl

Cutting mat

Thick fuse wire

Brass chain

Boning tool

Black outliner

White, royal blue, yellow, kelly green, light green and amber pearl paints

Royal blue, clear, orange, yellow and turquoise transparent paints

Fine brush

Clear pipe-and-peel paint

TECHNIQUES

2 How to outline, page 19

19 Photocopying an outline, page 30

21 Using self-adhesive lead, page 32

37 Solvent-based pearl paints, page 42

38 Solvent-based transparent paints, page 43

41 Pipe-and-peel paints, page 46

60 Cutting glass circles, page 59

ENLARGING THE TEMPLATE

Enlarge the template on a photocopier onto white paper first to get the size, then photocopy it onto the acetate. That way you don't waste any acetate.

---

1 Enlarge the template to the required size and photocopy it onto acetate. Lay one of the glass circles centrally over the design and draw round it onto the acetate.

2 Cut round the drawn line so that the acetate is the same size as the glass circles.

3 Lay the acetate on one glass circle, then lay the other glass circle on top of the acetate. Make sure that the design is positioned centrally.

4 Make a small mark where you want the top of the suncatcher to be.

5 Check that your lead is long enough to go right round the glass circles, with a little to spare.

6 Fold the length of lead in half and make a gentle crease at the middle. Lay the lead out flat on the cutting mat and, using the bradawl, make a hole about 5cm (2in) either side of the centre crease.

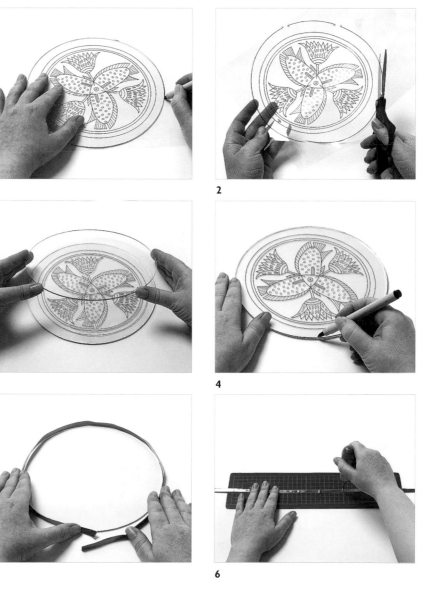

1

2

3

4

5

6

7 Cut a 8cm (3in) length of fuse wire and push half the length through one end of the chain. Twist it together close to the chain to form a loop. Make another loop the same at the other end of the chain. The lengths of wire should not be shorter than recommended or they may pull out when the suncatcher is hanging.

8 Peel the backing paper off the lead.

9 Push the ends of the wires through the holes in the lead. Open the ends out and press them down, either side of each hole, onto the sticky back of the lead.

10 Now position the centre crease in the lead against the pen mark at the top of the suncatcher. Hold the two circles of glass firmly together and start to stick down the lead. (If you are worried about the two circles slipping, then tape them together with masking tape. Remove the tape as you work round the suncatcher.) Position the lead centrally across the width of the two pieces of glass, bend the excess lead down over each side, onto the surface of the glass, and press it firmly in place. Self-adhesive lead is soft and easy to manipulate so this is difficult to do. Work from the centre round to one end of the lead, then go back to the centre and work round to the other end.

11 Overlap the ends of the lead just a little, then cut off any excess with scissors.

12 Using a boning tool, press the lead down onto the glass and run it around the edge. pressing down the wire under the lead.

13 On the back of the suncatcher, outline the main sections, or bolder lines, of the design.

14 Paint the design in sections, working on the middle first. Combine shades of the same colour and add highlights for a more painterly look. Leave it to dry. We painted the centre section in transparent paints.

15 Paint the remaining parts of the centre section next, then one of the outer rings. We used pearl paints on the two outer rings.

16 Paint the other outer ring. Finally, scribble clear pipe-and-peel onto the unpainted areas of glass for a textured finish.

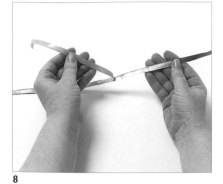

7

8

9

10

11

12

13

14

15

16

18 Winged mirror

We know that there is not much actual glass painting in this project; none at all, in fact. However, it is very striking and it will give you an opportunity to practice your metal leaf technique. If you really want to add colour, you could paint a border round the mirror. Enlarge the templates to the size you require and cut out the heart shape in mirror glass and the wings in plain glass.

MATERIALS

Heart shape cut from 4mm- (³⁄₁₆in-) thick mirror glass with two holes drilled near the top

Two wing shapes cut from 3mm- (¹⁄₈in-) thick plain glass

Heart and wing templates, page 151

Black pipe-and-peel outliner

Pink-toned metal leaf

Acrylic size

Fine brush

4mm- (³⁄₁₆in-) wide brass-coloured self-adhesive lead

Epoxy glue

Brass hooks and chain

TECHNIQUES

8 Pipe-and-peel outlining, page 22

9 Transferring designs onto mirror glass, page 24

21 Using self-adhesive lead, page 32

61 Cutting glass shapes, page 60

66 Using epoxy glue, page 62

92 Using metal leaf, page 82

1

2

4

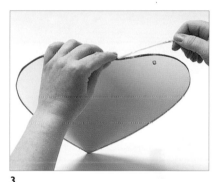

3

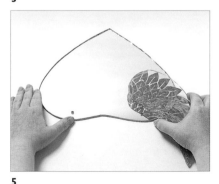

5

1 Enlarge the templates to the required size. Outline the design onto the wings and let them dry. Paint the feathers with acrylic size and lay metal leaf on top. Trim and brush away any excess leaf. Leave them to dry.

2 Peel off the outliner to reveal the feather design. Paint the wings with a coat of clear solvent-based transparent paint to seal them.

3 Stick brass-coloured self-adhesive lead right round the edge of the heart-shaped mirror.

4 Mix up epoxy glue and dab blobs onto the back of the inner part of one wing. Put the glue on areas gilded on the front and then it won't show.

5 Stick the wing to the mirror then repeat the process with the other wing, making sure they line up. Leave to dry then, put hooks through the drilled holes and hang the mirror from the chain.

19 Serving platter

The design possibilities for a plate are endless. We wanted this one to be practical and decorative, so we used air-drying polyester-based paints that allow the plate to be washed and warmed in an oven. We painted the design onto the back, so when you cut a cake on it you will not damage the paint. This is quite a complex design, but you could use the simpler one also given in the Motif Library.

We must have used all of the different paints in the air-drying polyester-based range: gels, transparents, pearls, shimmers. Some of the paints can be used straight from the bottle, while others are best brushed on or piped from an outlining bag. Experiment and see which you find easiest.

MATERIALS

Large glass plate

Thick brush

Fine brush

Surface conditioner

Cushion

Platter template, page 154

Air-drying polyester-based black outliner and paints

TECHNIQUES

2 How to outline, page 19

43 Air-drying polyester-based paints, page 48

1

2

3

4

5

6

7

1 Before you start you must give the glass a coat of the surface conditioner. Remember, you are working on the back of the plate, so this is the side you must coat.

2 Enlarge the template to the required size, cut it out and lay it on a cushion or folded-up piece of fabric. Lay the plate on top: the cushion will help to push the design up against the glass. Outline the design using the air-drying polyester-based outliner.

3 We used the air-drying polyester-based gels piped from an outlining bag first. Remember, as you are working on the back of the plate, you need to add the highlights first.

4 Then we squeezed the air-drying polyester-based transparent paint out of the tube, over the gel paints, so that the different textures show on the front of the plate.

5 If you are painting over any pre-painted areas or have not painted the glass for three or four hours. You will need to give it another coat of surface conditioner, otherwise the paint will not adhere to the glass.

6 We painted leaves in air-drying polyester-based gel, squeezed straight from the bottle.

7 We painted on the shimmer-finish air-drying polyester-based paints with a fine brush.

20 Layered picture frame

Don't attempt this project unless you have been good and have been practising outlining. A neat, straight line is what you need to be able to do for this project, so if you are not an expert when you start, you will be when you finish.

We knew the photograph that we wanted to frame and so we chose the colours of the gel paints to complement it. You can also make this project using different colours of outliner.

MATERIALS

Rectangle of 4mm- (³⁄₁₆in-) thick glass the size you want the finished frame to be

Rectangle of 2mm- (¹⁄₁₆in-) thick glass for the back, 1cm (½in) larger on three sides than the picture you want to frame

Line template, page 151

Four colours of gel paint to complement the picture you want to frame

Gold outliner

Rectangle of 4mm- (³⁄₁₆in-) thick glass the width of the frame by 10cm (4in) for the base

Ultra-violet glue

Ultra violet lamp

Four plastic bubble feet

Ruler

Pen

TECHNIQUES

2 How to outline, page 19

39 Gel paints, page 44

65 Using ultra-violet glue, page 62

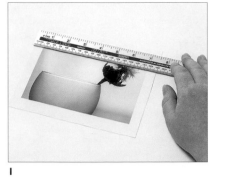

1

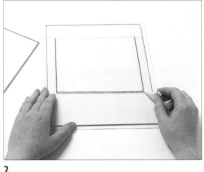

2

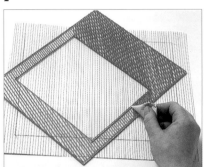

3

4

5

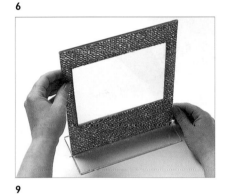

6

7

8

9

1 It is important that you measure the picture you want to frame before you cut the glass, as this project works best when the picture fits the frame exactly.

2 Make up a template for the frame by drawing round the main piece of glass on a sheet of white paper. Remove the large piece of glass and place the back piece on the paper where you want the picture to be in the finished frame. Use a ruler to make sure the back is central and then draw round it. Remove the back and lay the main piece back on the template. Fill an outlining bag with a light-coloured gel paint and outline round two sides and the bottom of the position of the back piece of glass.

3 When the paint is dry, turn the glass over on the template and outline right round the outside edge. Then, outline round all four sides

of the position of the back piece of glass.

4 Position the main piece of glass at an angle on top of the line template and, following the template lines carefully to keep them parallel, pipe across the frame with gel paint. Leave the outlined central area clear. Leave to dry for at least one hour.

5 Next, reposition the glass at a different angle on the line template and pipe over the first layer with another colour of gel paint. Leave to dry for an hour.

6 For the third layer we used gold outliner. Again, position the glass at a different angle. By now you probably won't be able to see the lines on the template through the layering, but you will be able to see where each line hits the side of the frame and where it re-emerges, which will help you to keep your lines straight. Continue building up

the layers; we piped six layers on this frame. When you have finished, leave it to dry at least overnight, or until the paint is hard.

7 Turn the picture frame over and outline a thin line of gel over the three lines you made in step 2.

8 Lay the back piece of glass onto the lines of wet gel. Leave it to dry.

9 Stick the frame to the middle of the base piece of glass with ultra-violet glue. When it is dry, stick a plastic bubble foot to each corner of the base. Slide the picture between the two pieces of glass at the back of the frame.

21 Gilded box

This is a wonderfully ornate-looking project, combining paint and gold metal leaf, but it is really quite simple to do, as all the panels are the same. For the handle and feet we used beautiful hand-made glass marbles, but you could also use glass nuggets.

If boxes are not your style, but you like this design, then make the project up without a lid and put a short candle inside to create a striking candle holder.

MATERIALS

Four 14cm (5½in) squares of 3mm- (⅛in-) thick glass for the sides

One 14cm (5½in) square of 3mm- (⅛in-) thick glass with a 1cm- (½in-) wide hole drilled in the middle for the lid

One 14cm (5½mm) square of 3mm- (⅛in-) thick glass with an 0.5cm- (¼in-) wide hole drilled in each corner for the base

Panel template, page 151

Black outliner

Gold leaf

Acrylic size

Fine brush

Shellac varnish

Red, orange, clear, royal blue, turquoise and purple solvent-based transparent paints

Epoxy glue

Cocktail stick

Masking tape

1 large marble for the handle

4 small marbles for the feet

Silicone glue

3mm- (⅛in-) wide self-adhesive brass-coloured lead

One 13cm (5in) square of 3mm- (⅛in-) thick glass

TECHNIQUES

2 How to outline, page 19

21 Using self-adhesive lead, page 32

38 Solvent-based transparent paints, page 43

58 Cutting straight lines in glass, page 58

62 Drilling holes in glass, page 60

66 Using epoxy glue, page 62

67 Using silicone glue, page 63

92 Using metal leaf, page 82

1

2

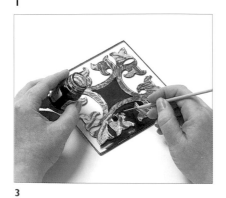

3

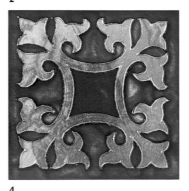

4

1 Outline the template onto the four sides and the lid. Paint acrylic size onto the pattern and cover it with gold metal leaf. Paint the whole base with size and cover it with leaf. Seal all the gilded areas with shellac varnish.

2 Paint the central area of the pattern with red, orange and clear transparent paints.

3 Paint around the outside of the pattern with royal blue, purple and clear transparent paints. Then let the panels dry completely.

4 The finished sides should look like this. The lid should look exactly the same but with a hole in the middle. (Before you paint the central part of the pattern on the lid, outline round the hole to stop the paint running into it.)

5 To stick the large marble to the lid, place it on the drilled hole in the glass.

6 Using masking tape, tape the marble tightly to the top of the lid.

7 Stick another length of tape over the marble at right angles to the first one and fold the ends over to the back to secure them. It is important that the marble is held firmly in place.

8 Mix up clear, two-part epoxy glue with a cocktail stick.

9 Lay the lid upside down on top of a wide-mouthed jar, so that it is flat. Fill up the drilled hole with the epoxy glue and leave it to dry. The glue will hold the marble in place.

10 Glue the feet to the base using the same method.

11 Now you can start assembling the box. Pipe a line of silicone glue down the edge of the glass sections that are to be stuck together.

12 Let the first two sides dry before you add the next two. Leave the box to dry completely.

13 Stick a length of brass-coloured self-adhesive lead to each edge of each side of the box. Stick another length around the top and bottom of the box and a length around the edge of the lid.

14 To make a lip on the inside of the lid (to prevent it sliding off), glue the 13cm (5in) square of plain glass centrally to the inside of the lid with blobs of epoxy glue on the back of the gilded areas of the lid, where they won't show.

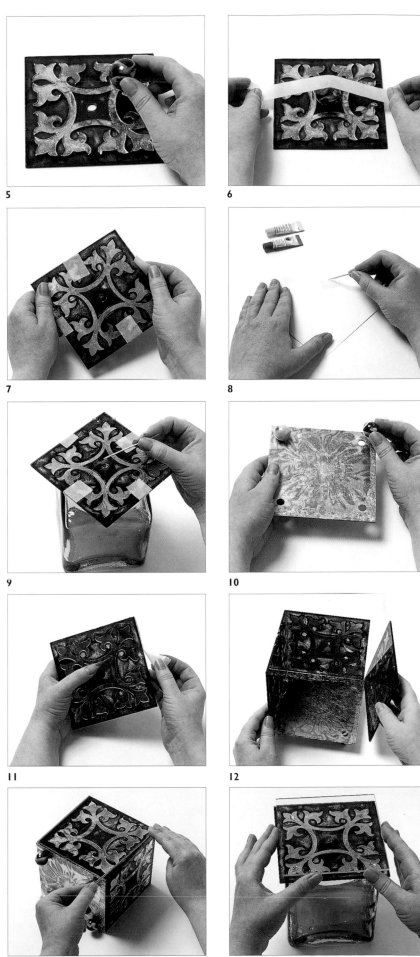

5

6

7

8

9

10

11

12

13

14

22 Arts and Crafts mirror

Painted mirrors look fantastic and demonstrate how you can easily make something very plain into a really eye-catching piece. We used self-adhesive lead instead of outlining to enhance the Arts and Crafts-style motifs, but you could just as easily outline the design. Alternatively, you could outline and paint the design onto self-adhesive film and stick this onto the mirror.

MATERIALS

A rectangular mirror the size required

Arts and Crafts mirror template,
page 151

Carbon paper

Pen

3mm- (⅛in-) wide self-adhesive lead

4mm- (³⁄₁₆in-) wide self-adhesive lead

Boning tool

Scalpel

Scissors

Fine brush

Red, kelly green and light green solvent-based transparent paints

Black and white solvent-based pearl paints

TECHNIQUES

9 Transferring designs onto mirror glass,
page 24

21 Using self-adhesive lead, page 32

37 Solvent-based pearl paints, page 42

38 Solvent-based transparent
paints, page 43

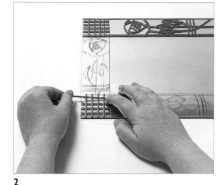
1

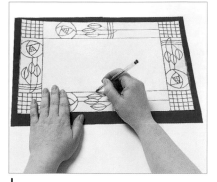
2

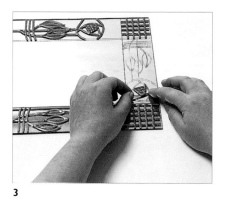
3

4

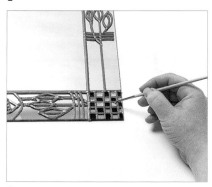
5

6

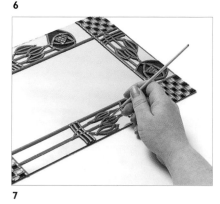
7

1 The top and side template sections is given on page 151. Enlarge them to fit your mirror, then copy them, cut out the sections and tape them together to make the whole template. Clean the mirror then transfer the design onto it.

2 Stick lead on one section of border at a time and complete it before you move on to the next section. Start with 3mm- (⅛in-) wide lead and the checkerboard corners of the design.

3 Move on to the flowers and work on the smallest parts first.

4 Use the 4mm- (³⁄₁₆in-) wide lead for the inner border lines. (There are no outer border lines as the mirror

frame will overlap the edges of the glass.) Remember to press all the lead, and particularly the joins, down well with the boning tool to stop the paint flowing underneath it.

5 When you have finished leading the mirror, clean it well to remove any finger marks and traces of carbon lines before painting it. Paint the checkerboard corners first. Paint alternate squares white, let them dry, then paint the remaining squares black.

6 Paint the flowers red.

7 Paint the leaves in a combination of kelly green and light green. Leave the paint to dry then fit the mirror into its frame.

23 Art Nouveau lamp

You can give old, and new, lamps the most amazing makeovers with glass paint. When you re-decorate a room, paint the old lamp to match the new colour scheme. Sometimes we see a lamp that is just crying out to be painted – like this one. We painted it in gel paints to give an old, hand-made glass effect and turned an inexpensive modern light into a classic piece. This project looks very hard and complicated to make, but it is, in fact, quite easy. Plan your colour scheme before you start and work around the lamp, painting a colour at a time, in a methodical way.

MATERIALS

Lamp with a glass shade

Black pipe-and-peel outliner

Sheets of flat glass

Flower and leaf templates, pages 152-153

Gel paints in your chosen colour scheme

Clear glass beads

TECHNIQUES

8 Pipe-and-peel outlining, page 22

39 Gel paints, page 44

87 Embedding objects in paint, page 78

1

2

1 Choose a lamp to paint. It must have a glass shade that is not too close to the bulb. If you can, take the shade off the lamp and work on it on a flat surface, you will find it mush easier to paint like this.

2 Enlarge or reduce the templates on page 152-153 to the sizes you want. Lay them under the sheets of flat glass and outline them. On the larger designs, make the outline fairly thick. Leave them to dry.

3 Peel the designs off the sheets of glass and stick them onto the lampshade. If you find that the outlining is not sticking to the glass (frosted glass, for example, is hard to stick outliner to), wipe the glass with damp kitchen paper, lay the outlining on the damp glass and pat it down with the damp cloth – it will stick then. Leave the glass to dry before you start to paint it.

3

4 Spend some time arranging the flowers and leaves on the lampshade. Place the larger designs on first, then fill in the gaps with the smaller ones. Remember that you can peel them off and re-position them if you want to.

5 Fill in any gaps between flowers by outlining simple leaf and flower shapes straight onto the glass. Also use the outliner to make centres for the small flowers.

6 Fill several outlining bags with different coloured of gel paints. Start to paint the flowers, mixing the colours straight onto the glass and working on one colour combination at a time. Paint all the flowers near the top of the lampshade that you want in the first colour combination, turning the shade as you work.

7 Put blobs of clear gel in the centres of some of the larger flowers and embed glass beads into them. When dry the paint will hold the beads firmly.

8 We find it best to finish all the painting at the top of the lampshade before moving down the sides. It is less messy this way.

9 Some of the smaller flowers can be painted in opaque gel paint to imitate opalescent glass.

10 Work round the lampshade and down the sides, painting all the flowers and leaves with gel paint. When they are all coloured, leave the lampshade to dry overnight.

11 Fill in the background gaps between the flowers and leaves with more gel paint. To work on the very edges of the lamp, lift it up and rest it on something substantial; we used a turntable but a big tin of paint would work well. As you add gel close to the edge, run your finger around the rim of the lampshade to smooth the paint.

4

5

6

7

8

9

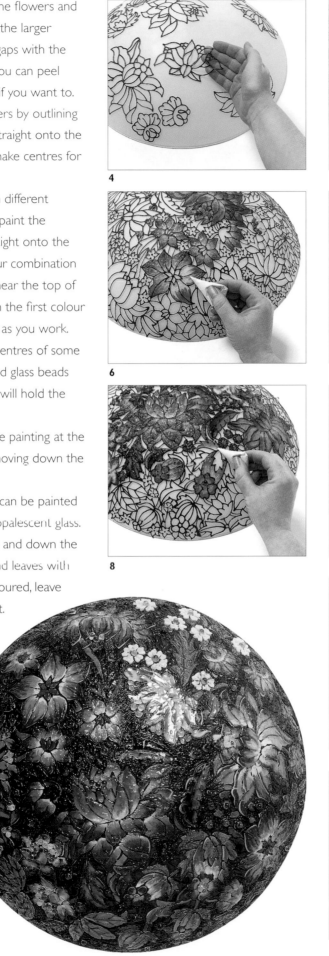

10

11

24 Three-dimensional balloon picture

We love making three-dimensional work: it taxes the brain when you are designing it, but the finished result is well worth the effort. If you hang it in a well-lit spot, not only do the angles change as you walk past, but the colours do as well. You can make a realistic picture with flowers, trees and hills fading into the distance, or you can use an abstract design to great effect.

We use a simple box frame, which makes it simple to assemble the sheets of glass into one picture, but if you use a different sort of frame, you may need to adapt the assembly instructions to suit it.

If you like this three-dimensional effect as much as we do, try making a coffee table or cupboard door – exactly the same principles apply. However, to cut down the weight we usually paint onto sheets of acrylic rather than glass when making larger items.

MATERIALS

Five sheets of 2mm ($\frac{1}{16}$in) glass to fit the picture frame

Three-dimensional balloon picture templates, four in total, page 155

Black outliner

Turquoise, purple, white, pale pink, cream, brown, amber, kelly green, light green and yellow solvent-based pearl paints

Fine brush

Gold outliner

Silicone glue

Box picture frame

One piece of mounting board to fit the frame, cut to leave a 2.5cm- (1in-) wide mount

Sheet of white paper to fit the frame

Masking tape

Wood glue

TECHNIQUES

2 How to outline, page 19

4 Over-outlining, page 20

37 Solvent-based pearl paints, page 42

67 Using silicone glue, page 63

PAINTING THE PICTURE

When we make three-dimensional pictures, the paints we use are determined by the design. Because balloons are not see-through, we used solvent-based pearl paints. But you can use any paints, or combinations of paints, that suit your design. Opaque and transparent paints look great when they overlap, as they change colour depending on the angle you look at the picture from.

1

2

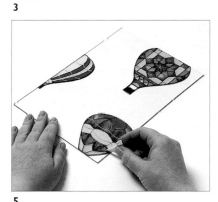

3

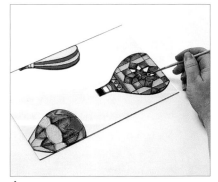

4

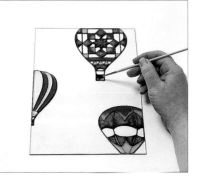

5

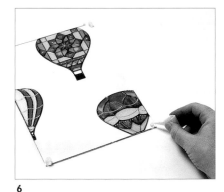

6

1 Outline one template onto each of the sheets of glass and leave them to dry.

2 Start painting the balloons in sections, painting the same coloured sections on each of the sheets of glass. We have worked on sheet one, the top sheet, in these steps, but the same principles apply to all the sheets. Use the finished shots of each sheet on page 139 to guide you as to what colours to use.

3 Continue to build up the colour on in sections at a time, and don't forget to paint the baskets.

4 Remember to leave the paint to dry on a section before you start painting one immediately adjacent to it.

5 Over-outline details onto the balloons with gold outliner.

6 There are various ways to separate the four sheets of glass within the picture. You can use glass beads or small nuggets, strips of wood or cardboard or plastic bubble feet. However, we prefer to use silicone glue. Pipe a tall blob of glue onto the front of each corner of each sheet, using a spiralling motion to make a blob a few millimetres high. When these blobs are dry they are rubbery and flexible, so if when assembling the frame, the stack of sheets of glass sits too high, you can squash it down a bit to fit it into the frame. Leave the glue to dry completely.

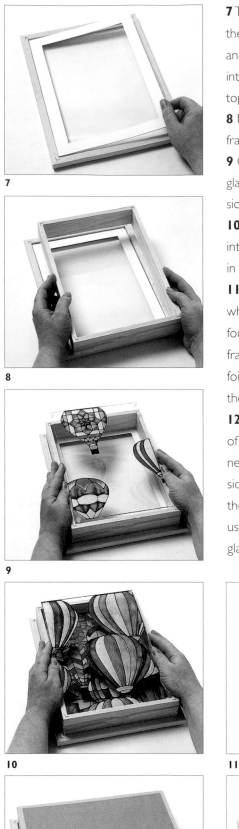

7 To assemble the picture, firstly place the front of the frame upside down and fit the unpainted sheet of glass into it. Lay the mounting board on top of this.

8 Next, place the box section of the frame on top of the front section.

9 Clean the first piece of painted glass, sheet one, and place it painted side down into the frame.

10 Fit each of the painted sheets into the frame, with sheet four going in last.

11 Place a piece of aluminium foil or white paper on the back of sheet four and place the back of the frame on top of this. The paper or foil will help to reflect light back into the picture.

12 Use masking tape to tape the back of the frame to the sides. Do this neatly, as the tape will show on the sides of the frame. We prefer to tape the back of the frame on, as if you use glue it can run down onto the glass inside and spoil the picture.

12

11

13

13 Run a line of wood glue down the rebate between the front and box sections of the frame. To make sure that they are securely glued together, push the box section as far as possible to one side on the front of the frame, run glue down the wider rebate, then push the box back and glue the other side. Repeat the process at the top and bottom of the frame then leave it to dry, making sure that the box central on the front of the frame.

DISPLAYING YOUR THREE-DIMENSIONAL PICTURE

If you leave the back off the picture you can hang it in a window so that it is lit from behind, or you can mount it a few centimetres (inches) away from a wall with a strip light behind it.

Alternatively you can ask a qualified electrician to put a light inside the frame. With the light shining through the glass from top to bottom it will look spectacular. However, please don't do what we once did, which was to run Christmas tree lights around the inside of the frame: they overheated and blew up. Be safe – ask a qualified electrician to install any lighting.

◁ Use these pictures of the painted sheets of glass to guide you in applying paint colours. Assemble the picture with sheet 1 at the front.

△ Sheet one

△ Sheet two

△ Sheet three

△ Sheet four

△ The assembled picture

MORE IDEAS

You don't have to use a box frame to make a three-dimensional picture. You can make a stand for a picture by cutting the appropriate number of evenly spaced grooves into two pieces of wood with a router. Simply slot the sheets of glass into the grooves. If you use this method, you don't need to put an unpainted sheet of glass at the front of the picture. The templates for this seahorse picture (four in total) are on page 157. We painted the seahorses with pearl paints, the seaweed with transparent paints and used small blobs of clear gel paint to make the air bubbles.

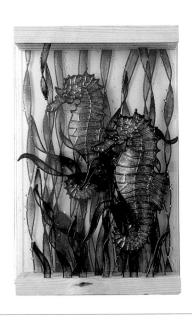

Motif library

In the first section of this library you will find all of the designs used in the projects: each one is labelled and any alternative motifs are supplied alongside. Also, scattered throughout the other sections, are the motifs used to illustrate some of the techniques.

We have included literally hundreds of motifs in this library, all ideally suited for glass painting. They are marshalled into five sections: Project Templates, Geometry and Symmetry, Birds and Beasts, Flowers and Foliage and Children's Designs. There are single and repeating designs, borders and corners, frames and centrepieces, intricate and simple motifs in many styles: in fact, something for everyone.

The motifs can be traced off or enlarged on a photocopier and used as templates for your own projects. There is plenty to choose from, so do make the most of them.

Project templates

△ 1 Honey-bee key cupboard, page 88

△ Alternative key cupboard design

△ 5 Contemporary painted table, page 98

△ 2 Celestial mobile, page 90 (four pieces)

△ 4 Decorated light bulb, page 96

△ 6 Koi carp vase, page 100   △ Alternative light bulb design   △ Alternative Koi carp design

△ 3 Modern mirror tiles, page 94 (five pieces)

▷ 7 Letter bottles, page 102

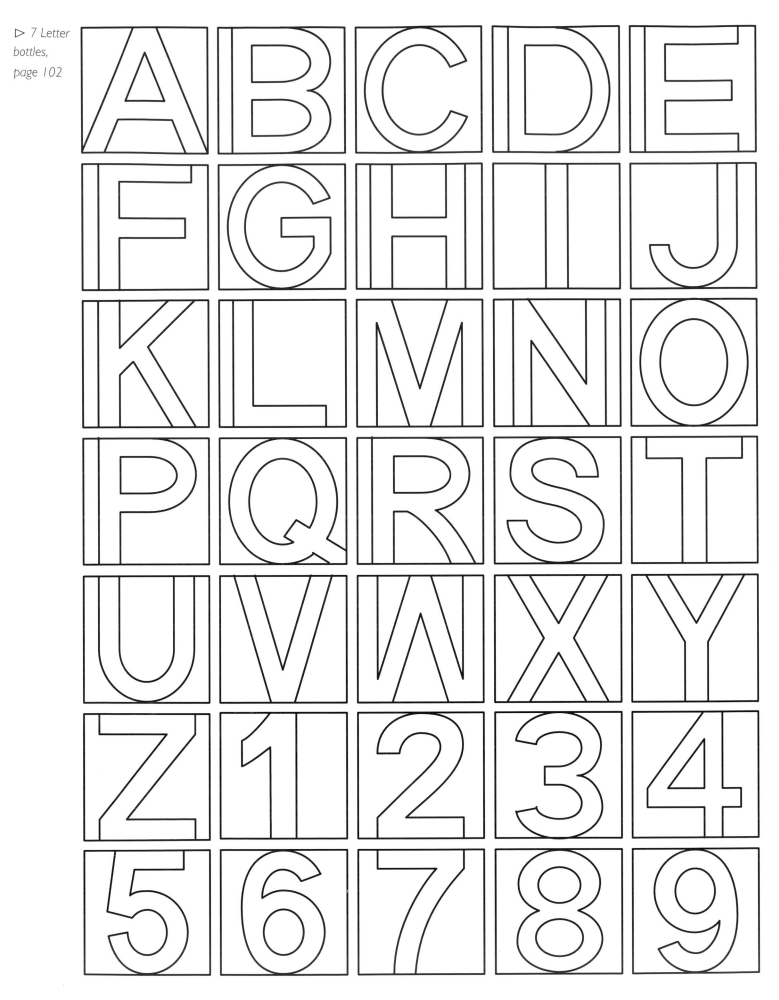

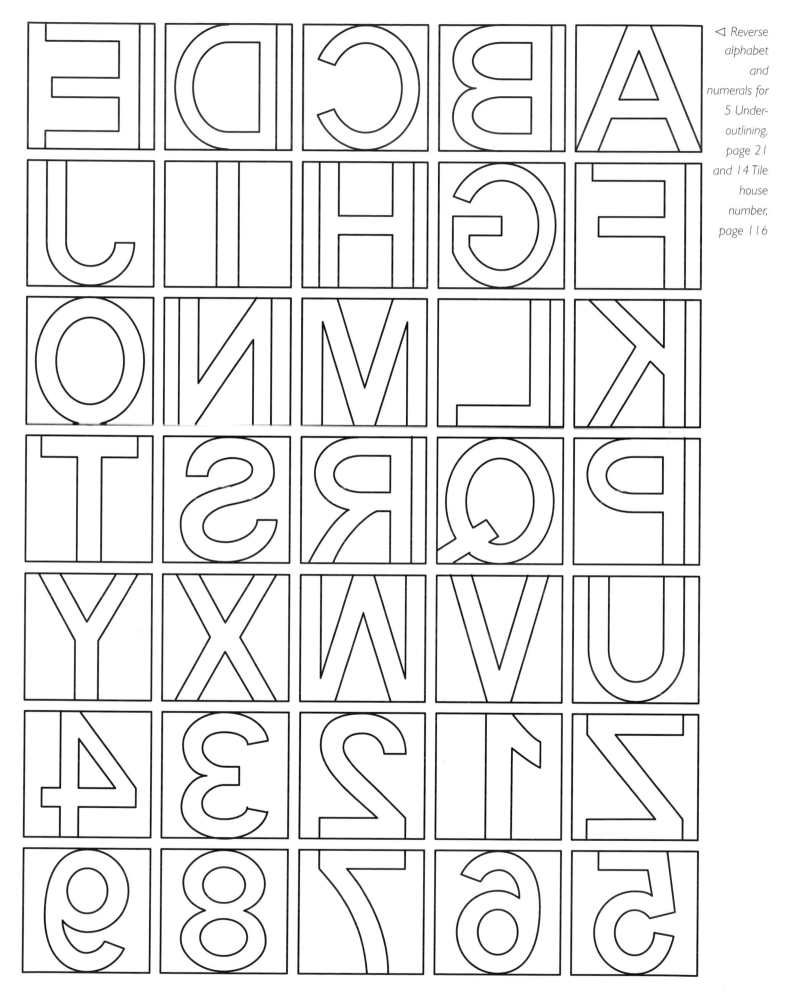

◁ Reverse alphabet and numerals for 5 Under-outlining, page 21 and 14 Tile house number, page 116

△ 8 Mosaic vase, page 104

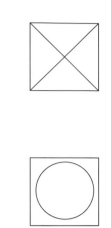

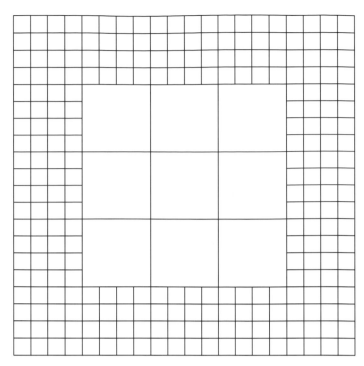

△ 9 Noughts and crosses board, page 106 (three pieces)

△ 10 Ocean aquarium, page 108

△ 12 Potted trees, page 112

△ ◁ ▷ Alternative tree designs

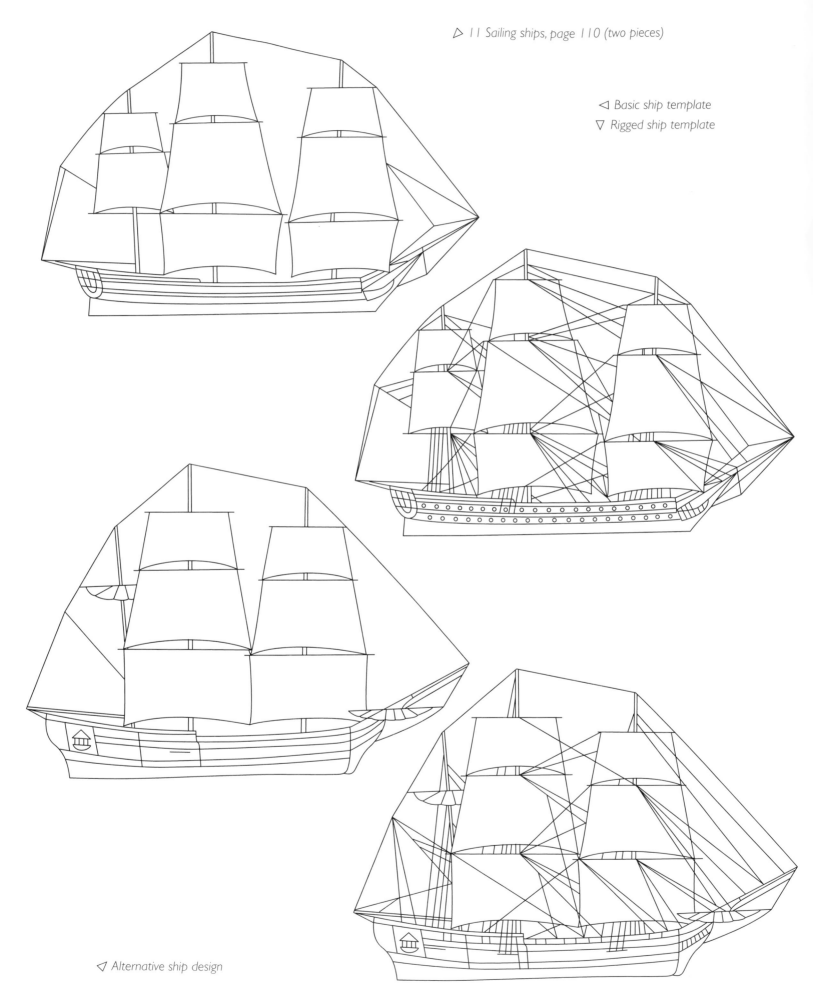

△ 11 Sailing ships, page 110 (two pieces)

◁ Basic ship template
▽ Rigged ship template

◁ Alternative ship design

△ Alternative ship design

▽ Alternative ship design

▷ ▽ 13 Mirrored candle sconce, page 114 (5 pieces)

▷ Alternative candle sconce design

◁ Alternative candle sconce designs

▷ Alternative candle sconce design

△ 14 Tile house number, page 116

△ 17 Suncatcher, page 122

△ Top template

△ 15 Etched coasters, page 118 (twelve pieces)

△ Bottom template

16 Art Deco clock, page 120 (six pieces)

▽ 22 Arts and Crafts mirror, page 132

△ 21 Gilded box, page 130

△ 20 Layered picture frame, page 128

△ ◁ 18 Winged mirror, page 125 (three pieces)

23 Art Nouveau lamp, page 134 (thirty three pieces)

△ 19 Serving platter, page 126

◁ Alternative serving platter design

24 Three-dimensional balloon picture, page 136

Alternative three-dimensional picture design

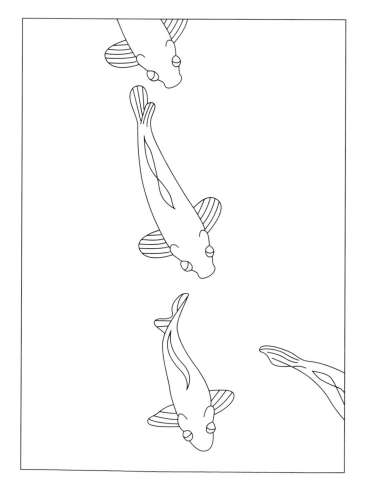

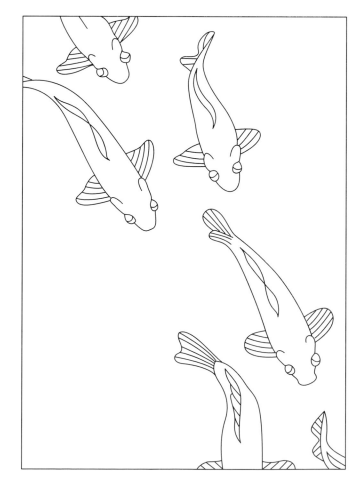

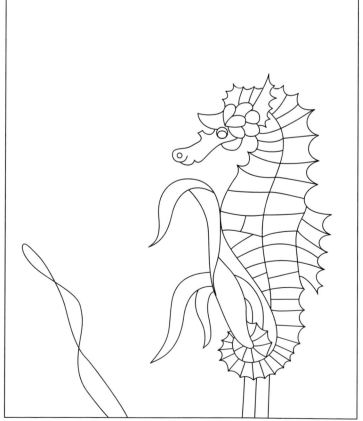

Geometry and symmetry

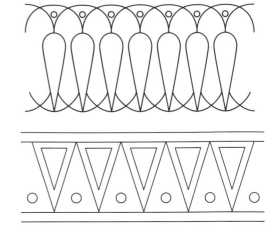

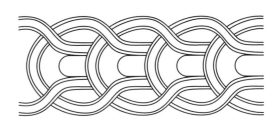

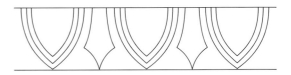

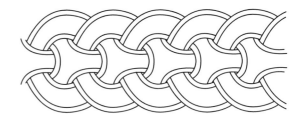

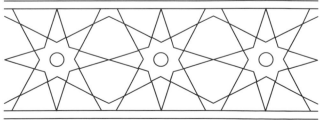

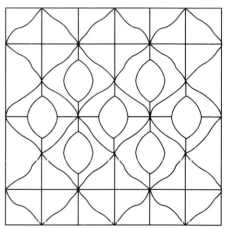

Birds and beasts

Flowers and foliage

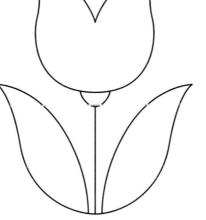

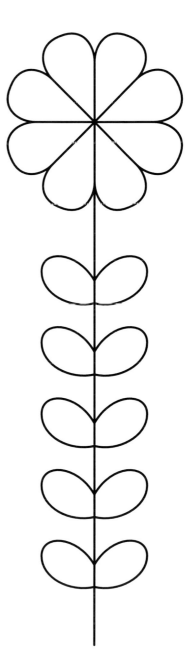

Children's designs

Suppliers

Rainbow Glass
85 Walkden Road
Worsley
Manchester M28 7BQ
England
Tel: 0161-790 3025
Fax: 0161-661 5787
E-mail: rainbowglass@aol.com
Website:
www.rainbowglasspaints.com
By mail order: outliners, self-adhesive lead, solvent-based transparent paints, solvent-based pearl paints, water-based paints, pipe-and-peel paints, light bulb paints, luminous paints, glass-painting films, etching creams, designs, glass blanks, glass-painting videos. Call for details of glass-painting workshops. For distributors of Rainbow Glass products in the USA and Canada, contact Rainbow Glass in the UK.

UK

Amaco Europe Ltd
PO Box 467, Longton
Stoke on Trent ST11 9BE
Tel: 01782-399219
Fax: 01782-394891
E-mail: sales@amaco.co.uk
Website: www.amaco.co.uk
Metal cream and metal paints.

Design Objectives
36/44 Willis Way
Fleets Industrial Estate
Poole, Dorset BH15 3TB
Tel: 01202-679976
Fax: 01202-672972
E-mail: info@designobjectives.com
Air-drying polyester-based paints.

Edding (UK) Ltd
The Merlin Centre
Acrewood Way
St Albans
Herts AL4 0JY
Tel: 01727-846688
Fax: 01727-839970
E-mail: emmalloyd@edding.co.uk
Website: www.edding.de
Outliners, glass paints.

George Weil Ltd
Old Portsmouth Road
Peasmarsh
Guilford GU3 1LZ
Tel: 01483-565800
Fax: 01483-565807
E-mail: sales@georgeweil.co.uk
Outliners, glass paints.

House of Marbles
The Old Pottery
Pottery Road
Bovey Tracey
Devon TQ13 9DS
Tel: 01626-835358
Fax: 01626-835315
E-mail:
uk@houseofmarbles.uk.com
Website:www.houseofmarbles.uk.com
Glass shapes and marbles.

Pebeo (UK) Ltd
109 Solent Business Centre
Millbrook Road West
Millbrook
Southampton SO15 0HW
Tel: 023-8090 1914
Fax: 023-8090 1916
E-mail: pebeouk@aol.com
Website: www.pebeo.com

Outliners, glass paints, oven-bake outliners and paints, water-based paints and gels.

Plaid Enterprises
21 Chestnut Drive
Poynton
Cheshire SK12 1QG
Tel: 01625-266929
Fax: 01625-266868
E-mail: lgallonplaid@cwcom.net
Website: www.plaidonline.com
Water-beased paints and outliners, pipe-and-peel paints.

Staedtler (UK) Ltd
Pontyclun
Mid Glamorgan CF72 8YJ
Tel: 01443-237421
Fax: 01443-228052
E-mail:
marketinguk@staedtler.com
Website: www.staedtler-uk.co.uk
Outliner pens, metal leaf.

USA

Amaco Inc
4717 West 16th Street
Indianapolios
Indiana 46222
Tel: 317 244 6871
Fax: 317 248 9300
E-mail: enquiries.amaco.com
Website: www.amaco.com
Metal cream and metal paints.

Decart Inc
PO Box 309
Morrisville
Vermont 05661
Tel: 802 888 4217
Fax: 802 888 4123

E-mail: dekapaint@pwsshift.com
Outliners, glass paints, light bulb paints.

Delta Technical Coatings
2550 Pellissier Place
Whittier
CA 90601-1505
Tel: 1-800 423 4135/
562 695 7969
Fax: 562 695 5805
E-mail: advisor@deltacrafts.com
Website: www.deltacrafts.com
Outliners, glass paints, air-drying polyester-based paints, frosting paints.

Eastern Art Glass
PO Box 128
Wyckoff
New Jersey 07481
Tel: 1-800 872 3458
Fax: 201 847 0231
E-mail: etchgal@idt.net
Website: www.etchworld.com
Etching cream and stencils.

House of Marbles
PO Box 247
11/3 Ilene Court
Bellemead
New Jersey 08502
Tel: 908 281 9158
Fax: 908 281 9198
E-mail:
usa@houseofmarbles.uk.com
Website:
www.houseofmarbles.uk.com
Glass shapes and marbles.

Pebeo (USA and Canada)
1905 Rue Roy
Sherbrooke
QC J1K 2X5
Tel: 819 829 5012
Fax: 819 821 4151
E-mail: pebeo@globetrotter.net
Outliners, glass paints, oven-bake
outliners and paints, water-based
paints and gels.

Staedtler Inc
21900 Plummer Street
Chatsworth
CA 91311
Tel: 818 882 6000
Fax: 1-800 675 8124
E-mail: www.custserv@staedtler-use.com
Website: www.staedtler-usa.com
Outliner pens, metal leaf.

Plaid Enterprises – United States
3225 Westech Drive
Norcross
GA 30092
Tel: 1-800 392 8673
E-mail: glasstohelp-glasscrafting@plaidonline.com
Website: www.plaidonline.com
Water-based paints and outliners,
pipe-and-peel paints.

Yorkshire Leaded Glass
120 Georges Road
New Brunswick
New Jersey 08901
Tel: 732 247 7656
Fax: 732 247 7659
Self-adhesive lead, glass bevels.

Some of the designs in the Motif Library on pages 140–189 are selected from *The Crafter's Pattern Sourcebook* by Mary MacCarthy, published by Collins & Brown

Author's acknowledgements

We would like to thank the following for all their help and support in the writing of this book. Alan Hall, Dawn Little, Keith Illingworth, Andrew Raymond, Bob Prentice, Steve Pidd, Joy Freestone, John Falder, Alan McColl, Daler Rowney, Jan Pack, Jan Schield, Roger Daniels – our designer, Kate Haxell – our editor, Matt Dickens – our photographer. We would like to say a special thank you to Paul and Angie Boyer of *The Craftsman Magazine* for all their support. There have been so many other people who have given us help that there is really not room to mention them all, but thank you anyway.

Index